NEWARK PUBLIC LIBRARY
5 2125 300742360

W9-AEE-710

"The 'protectors' of Marwencol returning from a patrol and re-entering my town."

"This is a photo of the 1942–43 New Year's Eve party in the Ruined Stocking Catfight Club in Marwencol, Belgium."

"Five SS soldiers sneak up and attack me, punching and kicking at my head."

Welcome to

MARK HOGANCAMP
& CHRIS SHELLEN

WENCOL

PRINCETON ARCHITECTURAL PRESS
NEW YORK

BUZZ

"Pvt. Mel takes a break to go fishing."

by

Tod Lippy

Esopus Magazine

In 2005 I was at a party in the West Village when a friend of mine, David Naugle, said he had something he wanted to show me. Taking me aside, he pulled out his laptop and began scrolling through scans of astonishing photographs: striking, cinematic images of military figurines and Barbie dolls—or wait, were they actual people?—waging pitched, bloody battles, socializing in a bar, or simply engaging in everyday activities, such as driving, petting a dog, or cuddling a teddy bear.

I was transfixed: who made these? David told me it was a neighbor of his, Mark Hogancamp, whom he had first noticed walking back and forth on Route 213 in Upstate New York, pulling a scale-model military jeep along the shoulder of the road. I turned to David and said, "Have you shown these to anyone else?" When he said no, I had only two words for him: "Please don't."

A few weeks later, I went with David to meet Mark at his place upstate. I instantly understood where the intensity of vision so apparent in these gripping photographs came from: Mark was focused on, and immersed in, every aspect of an imaginary town he had constructed from scratch and was now documenting with an old 35 mm camera.

Mark gave us a tour of this town, Marwencol—the church, Pocket Full of Posies, and, inside his house in a spare bedroom, the Ruined Stocking Catfight Club. He proudly pointed out every item on and behind the bar, from tiny handcrafted signs, letting patrons know that catfights were staged, to a variety of barware, each glass and pitcher modified by Mark to appear as realistic as possible. By the time we left, I was exhilarated and deeply moved—a response I have encountered only rarely in the hundreds of visits to artists' studios I've made over the years.

The beauty of doing a small, nonprofit arts magazine on your own is that everything can happen very quickly—there aren't layers of editors, art directors, and publishers to pitch to and wait for a green light from, and there is greater flexibility with deadlines, space constraints, and many other pitfalls common in commercial publishing. We ran Mark's "Marwencol on My Mind"—featuring fifteen of his photographs, along with

A.

B.

an interview of Mark by David—just a few months later, in *Esopus* 5 (fall 2005). It remains one of the pieces in *Esopus* of which I am most proud.

It's a little too easy to group Mark with other respected contemporary artists who incorporate dolls into their photo-based work, such as Laurie Simmons and David Levinthal. What makes Mark's photographs so unique is the utter lack of irony he employs in his utilization of Dragon Models Limited military figurines, Barbie dolls, and movie action figures. There is no distance between Mark and these subjects, no *wink-wink* moment between him and the viewer. The fact that we invest so heavily in his work is not only a testament to Mark's fertile imagination, obsessive attention to detail, and exquisite visual sensibility; it is a testament to his own emotional investment in Marwencol and the lives of its ever-expanding group of inhabitants.

To me, Mark is the ultimate artist: completely devoid of cynicism and utterly immune to the machinations of the art market, he reserves all of his energy and ambition for the work itself. He is one of the few creative people I know who views his practice as not only fulfilling but also totally sustaining.

Through Marwencol, Mark has regained his cognitive faculties, reengaged on his own terms with a world that all but tossed him aside, and graced that world with a truly unique vision. We are all better for having experienced Marwencol through his eyes.

A. Mark giving a tour of Marwencol in 2005. (photo by David Naugle)
B. Mark with *Esopus* editor Tod Lippy at White Columns Gallery in 2006. (photo by Tom Putnam)

"My friend Jeff helps his wife, Chris, down a bump in the path. They're on their way back from a photo shoot at Marwencol Falls."

"Medi-Jeep tries to save one of the Rangers who was hit by a sniper on New Year's Day."

Part I

MARK'S STORY

First Life

"Before the attack, I think I was a lot happier... a lot more happy-go-lucky and innocent and comical. // I used to be able to draw. I would see something and I could draw it on paper like I was following an outline. I thought I was gonna make it as an illustrator...I illustrated two children's books before the attack, in between my drinking stints. // I could play guitar and sing too. I was in three bands...all punk rock bands. I could play every instrument except lead guitar. But I was drunk all the time, like Keith Richards—always knocking over the drum set. // If the attack had never happened, I would probably still be a drunk, drinking a half gallon of whiskey a day, turning more yellow than I already was. I would've died...maybe been hit by a train or something. // It's kind of ironic. My higher power meant well, but while that door was open, while it was extracting the alcoholism from me, it took other things too. Drawing, guitar playing, dancing, walking, talking. I can't remember any Christmases or graduation. // It's all gone. That guy is gone."

Mark Edward Hogancamp was born in 1962 in a middle-class suburb of Newburgh in Upstate New York. His parents were a study in opposites—his father, Paul Hogancamp, was a gruff blue-collar man; his mother, Edda Homuth, an elegant, young German woman.

Mark was their firstborn, the eldest of three sons. He was a sunny and gracious boy who spent most of his time inside his imagination. His mother claimed, "He could look up in the sky and make up a story."

Mark's stories usually starred well-defined characters based on family members and friends. Even as a boy, he had an innate eye for character and could imitate anyone around him—man or woman—from their accent to the smallest physical mannerism.

Like many children, Mark also loved to draw. And once again, his keen eye for detail produced unusual results.

In 1968 Edda received a call from Mark's kindergarten teacher, who had given the class an assignment to draw a picture of their parents. Most of the drawings looked the same—Dad was a stick figure; Mom wore a triangle dress and had corkscrew hair. But Mark's drawing was different. For a start, his parents actually looked like people. They had fleshy arms and realistic faces. They were also totally naked. Paul had a penis and Edda had breasts. Mark's teacher was concerned, but Edda, who had more European sensibilities, found it charming.

"I realized very early that Mark was creative and different," she said. "And I mean 'different' in a good way. He was interested in things that others just did not notice."

One such object of Mark's fascination was his maternal grandfather, "Papi." Papi had lost a leg in World War II, and he told exciting tales of heroic battles in faraway places. What made Papi's stories unique was that he had fought under Adolf Hitler during the war.

Like many members of Germany's *Wehrmacht* (German armed forces), Papi did not personally support Hitler or his mission. But he had the misfortune of completing his training as a mechanic at the very beginning of the war. He was immediately conscripted into the *Luftwaffe* (German air force) as an antiaircraft artillery mechanic.

Papi's stories left Mark with an interesting perspective on the war. Mark still viewed the Allied forces as the heroes of the story and Hitler's *Schutzstaffel* (the cold-blooded SS) as the villains. But he considered the everyday soldiers in Germany's Wehrmacht to be regular people. Some were bad, but some were decent men caught on the wrong side of history.

opposite: Mark as a young boy with his mother and younger brother Mike.

A.

B.

As Mark grew older, he became the kid in the back of class who furiously doodled while the teacher was talking. His grades were average, but his artistic technique was blossoming. Like a boardwalk caricaturist, he could capture his friends and family members with just a few strokes of his pen. It also gave him a visual outlet for the darker thoughts in his head—aggressive scenes of violence and war.

In the early 1980s, after a few mediocre years of high school and community college in Poughkeepsie, New York, Mark followed in his friends' footsteps and enlisted in the US Navy. Officially, he was a boatswain's mate in charge of steering and refueling ships. Unofficially, he became his ship's illustrator, capturing scenes and storylines—some real, some imaginary—from life on the ship and different ports of call. He traveled throughout Europe—to Spain and Italy and France—but ironically never made it to Belgium, where he would eventually set his 1:6 scale world.

On the seemingly auspicious date of August 4, 1984 (8/4/84), Mark married his girlfriend, Anastasia, while he was still in the service. Anastasia

A. A 1984 sketch by Mark during his time in the US Navy.
B. A note to his fiancé, Anastasia, from Mark's 1983 navy diary.

C.

D.

was a Russian Polish girl he'd met back in the student lounge of Dutchess Community College. Their relationship was exciting and tumultuous, kept alive through a cycle of longing during Mark's tours of duty and electric homecomings.

Five years later, Mark left the military with an honorable discharge. Trapped at home with a wife he barely knew and no military regimen to keep his mind occupied, he began to drink heavily. Anastasia's frustration grew. Eventually she left him, and Mark's life started on a bumpy downward spiral.

In the early 1990s, Mark found a good job building showrooms for trade shows but soon lost it. He took out his anger in mosh pits at local punk clubs, until he was arrested for drunk driving and forced to give up his car because he couldn't afford the insurance. He was homeless for a while, living in a tent, and was finally jailed for drunkenly showing up at his girlfriend's house with a 12-gauge shotgun he was using as a crutch.

The judges could see that Mark wasn't a bad guy; he was just a lost boy with a crippling addiction. So Mark found himself in rehab over and

C. A 1995 diary sketch of Mark being sentenced to jail.
D. A 1995 self-portrait of Mark homeless, sleeping in the woods.

... A WAR STORY ...

BY M.E. HOGANCAMP
BMSN - USN

1984 - DECEMBER - 29

A short illustrated story from Mark's 1983–87 diary in which a World War II British RAF pilot decides to spare the life of a German pilot in a crippled Heinkel aircraft.

over again. He went to AA, veterans' services, self-help groups, a Catholic monastery—anywhere that offered answers. But every time a program ended, he wound up at home with a bottle in his hands.

Eventually, Mark took a job as a kitchen worker in the last place an active alcoholic should probably work—a restaurant with a bar. He frequently called in "sick" to his job at the Anchorage Restaurant in Kingston, New York, and smelled like liquor, but he was a decent guy and he never drank at work, so his boss kept him around.

By day, Mark swept and mopped the floors, made meatballs for the spaghetti, scraped pans, and took out the trash. After work, he rode his bike home, closed the blinds, and opened a bottle. He preferred to drink at home—a half gallon of vodka interspersed with full glasses of water that probably saved his liver. Then he'd play guitar and sing, watch TV, write in his journal, and pass out.

In his more sober moments, Mark continued to sketch in his journal and paint extraordinarily realistic military miniatures, which he gave to friends and occasionally sold through Kingston's J&J's Hobbies. He also indulged in another private, lifelong passion: cross-dressing.

His mother knew about his lifestyle, and while she didn't encourage it, she felt she understood it. "He loves women...the beauty of women," she said. "And I think in a way he does it because he loves the feminine so much. It's not that he ever wanted to be a woman. It's not that he is gay. I think it's a compliment to women."

To Mark, it just felt good. He was lonely. In his mind, no girl would want an alcoholic with no prospects. But when he put on women's things—hose, heels, nail polish, perfume—he felt close to them.

For nearly ten years, Mark's life continued in this pattern—go to work, go home, get drunk, draw, dress up, pass out. While everyone else was out celebrating the new millennium, Mark was home alone...a thirty-eight-year-old divorced, alcoholic kitchen worker living on state assistance. He hated it. He hated himself and his dependence on alcohol. He prayed to God to take it all away. And He did.

opposite: "My Last Drunk," a sketch drawn just a few months before the attack.

"MY LAST DRUNK"

CHAPTER TWO

The Attack

"I walked up to the bar—the place my friends had invited me to—and when I got there, they weren't there. I figured, I'm not walking all the way home. I'm gonna sit and have a drink. And that's the last memory I have. // I had to find out from other people what happened to me. I know I was pushed down from behind and kicked, but I can only imagine what was done to me that night from stories I've heard. // I do believe that I died that night. People ask me what it's like to die, because I believe that I died there in Kingston Hospital and they brought me back. // My brother, the cop, asked me if I saw any lights or if I heard any voices, and I told him, no. It was dark. It was silent. It was nothing. No lights. No music. No people. I didn't hover over my body in a corner of a room. Nothing. It was just... it wasn't cold. It wasn't warm. It was just quiet. Peace. It was darkness."

opposite: A soldier is killed during a New Year's patrol of Marwencol.

Friday, April 7, 2000

On Friday, April 7, 2000, Mark was working his shift at the Anchorage. Owner Julie Swarthout, bartender Tom Neubauer, and some friends were making plans to check out the karaoke night at a local bar called the Luny Tune Saloon after work. Like always, they invited Mark along. And like always, he declined. Mark preferred to drink alone.

Several hours later, Julie and the others stepped into the darkness of the Luny Tune and felt immediately uneasy. The patrons seemed rude and there was something off about the atmosphere, so they left to find another bar.

Meanwhile, after a few drinks at home, Mark finally worked up the courage to join his friends. He pulled on a Harley-Davidson shirt, his white sailor cap, and a black leather jacket with an American flag on the back and made his way down to the bar, arriving at around 10:00 p.m. He'd just missed his friends.

Mark didn't have a cell phone to call them, so he sat down at the bar and ordered his signature drink, a boilermaker—"a shot of whiskey and a hug of beer." He emptied one after the other for the next four hours.

Saturday, April 8, 2000

At around 1:30 a.m., Mark got into a conversation with a lanky twenty-three-year-old blond guy named Freddy Hommel, who was sitting at the bar. The conversation got off to a spirited start. Both Hommel and Mark were of German ancestry, so they talked about their heritage and tossed around a few German words. The bartender heard Hommel joke about "Nazism, Hitler, [he] said something about swastikas, just generally joking around and laughing." Then the mood changed.

A few people overheard Mark reveal to Hommel that he was a cross-dresser. The conversation grew awkward; Hommel looked upset.

Across the room, Hommel's friend Richard Purcell, twenty-one years old, was standing with a group of friends by an arcade game. He recognized the look on Hommel's face; he'd seen it before—usually before a fight. His friends "Black Freddy," sixteen years old, David Mead, nineteen years old, and Noah Rand, also twenty-one years old, spotted it too. Black Freddy walked over to Hommel twice to tell him to calm down.

The conversation continued for a few minutes until Hommel stood up and ordered another drink. The bartender refused—closing time—so Hommel grabbed his friends and walked out to smoke by the side of the

opposite: A police photo from the scene of Mark's attack on April 8, 2000.
(photo provided by the Ulster County Sheriff's Office)

building. Mark walked out after them but returned a few seconds later to grab his jacket, which he'd left on a chair. He was visibly drunk (medical records later listed his blood alcohol level at over 0.30), so the bartender asked if he needed a ride. Mark said no thanks, he'd walk home.

It was about 2:10 in the morning. Mark walked outside and talked for a minute with Hommel and his friends as they smoked. Purcell later claimed that Hommel was taunting Mark, trying to get him to say something offensive, something about hating black people, like Black Freddy. But Mark didn't take the bait.

"Hey man," he said, "I don't hate anybody. Everyone's cool."

A minute or two later, the bartender glanced through the glass panels of the front door and saw Mark walk toward the street. Trailing behind him was Hommel. Hommel let Mark walk a few yards down the street and then, when Mark wasn't looking, he charged.

Hommel ran at Mark and rammed into him with his shoulder, tackling him to the ground. The guys heard an audible thump when Mark's head hit the pavement, and he was out cold. Then Hommel started swinging.

This was Hommel's fight. None of his friends had a problem with Mark, but there's an unwritten code among guys like Purcell and Hommel: if your friend gets into a fight, you have his back. So the four ran over and jumped in.

Later on, each of them would tell authorities that they kicked less than everyone else and were more concerned about Mark than the others. The only thing they agreed on was that Mead and Rand didn't jump in with quite the same enthusiasm as Hommel, Purcell, and Black Freddy.

While Mead and Rand kicked at Mark's legs, Black Freddy later told detectives that he, Hommel, and Purcell stomped repeatedly on Mark's head and chest with their boots.

Purcell claimed that Black Freddy punted the right side of Mark's face like a football two or three times, knocking it back and forth. Then he and Hommel joined in, ultimately smashing in Mark's right eye.

The whole fight only lasted a minute or so, but Mark's face had been destroyed and he wasn't fighting back. That scared Mead and Rand. They dragged the others into their two cars and sped off, leaving Mark unconscious and bleeding in the middle of the road. At about the same time, a local bartender named Nora Noonan was just ending her shift at nearby Riccardi's Hideaway. She picked up her daughter at a friend's house and headed home. It was a little after 2:30 a.m., about twenty minutes after the attack. As they turned onto Lincoln Street, they saw what looked like a black garbage bag in the middle of the street. No…it was a man.

Noonan drove around Mark to a nearby diner to look for a pay phone but couldn't find one. So she pulled out and parked in front of Mark to protect him from traffic.

Noonan and her daughter ran over and shook Mark, but he didn't respond. He looked terrible—his eyes were swollen shut, his breathing was ragged, and he had what looked like a tire track across his forehead. Noonan assumed he'd been run over, not knowing that the tire track was actually a boot print.

Noonan raced over to the Luny Tune and banged on the door. Finally, the bartender and the owner answered. Noonan told them about the guy in the street, and the bar's owner muttered, "Those darn kids."

The group ran back to Mark, and Noonan noticed he wasn't breathing anymore. So they rolled him over onto his side and blood came spilling out of his nose and mouth. If that blood had blocked his breathing for even a minute or two longer, Mark would have died.

The bar's owner called 911, and paramedics sped Mark over to the ER at Kingston Hospital. He was in respiratory failure. With only minutes to spare, Dr. Joel Ginsberg and his team vacuumed the blood from Mark's throat, intubated him, and put him on a ventilator to get him breathing again.

A CT scan of Mark's head showed that Mark's five attackers had completely destroyed the bony cavity that supported his right eye. It would need to be reconstructed, or Mark's eye would sink into his sinus cavities, leaving him disfigured and potentially blind in that eye.

That level of surgery was well beyond the capabilities of Kingston's ER, so Dr. Ginsberg had Mark transferred to Westchester Medical Center, in Valhalla, New York.

It was now late morning on Saturday, April 8. While Mark was being moved to Westchester Medical, Purcell was heading home, having just walked his pregnant girlfriend to work. Along the way, he spotted a friend of his named Steve and flagged him down. Steve had been at the Luny Tune the night before but had left with a girl before the fight began.

Purcell told Steve about how he and his friends had "stomped [Mark] and just kept stomping him, on his head." As proof, Purcell showed Steve the dried blood on his boots. Then he asked if Steve wanted to hang out

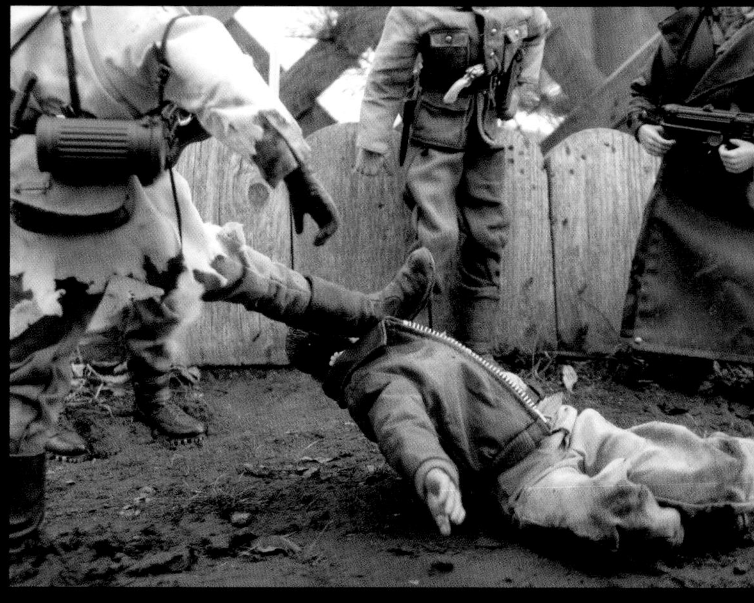

Photos illustrating a Marwencol story in which Mark's alter ego, Hogie, is nearly beaten to death by five SS soldiers.

at a party that night. Steve said Purcell seemed normal, "like happy Richie… how he always acted."

Over at Westchester Medical, Mark's family was finally admitted to his room in intensive care after hours of waiting. His mother was horrified by what she saw. "There was really no way I could have recognized Mark," she recalled. "I knew his hands and feet, but his face was just a swollen, purple mess."

In preparation for surgery on his eye, Mark was placed in a medically induced coma. At first, his body reacted badly; he jerked involuntarily and his vitals were unsteady. Doctors were stumped until Mark's friend Tom told them that Mark was an alcoholic. After just a day in intensive care without alcohol, his body was going through withdrawal.

Sunday, April 9, 2000

While doctors stabilized Mark, Ulster County detectives began to round up the suspects.

Rand and Mead each claimed to have not taken part in the beating. Purcell and Black Freddy confessed to some violence, but both placed the blame squarely on Hommel, who had become upset after Mark revealed that he was a cross-dresser.

Hommel initially joked around with detectives, calling himself a karaoke superstar. Then he defended his actions by claiming Mark was a "cross-dressing murderer"—a neo-Nazi who thought POWs deserved to die. He told detectives that Mark had threatened to kick his ass; he thought Mark

Mug shots of Freddy Hommel (left) and Richard Purcell soon after the attack. (photos provided by the Ulster County Sheriff's Office)

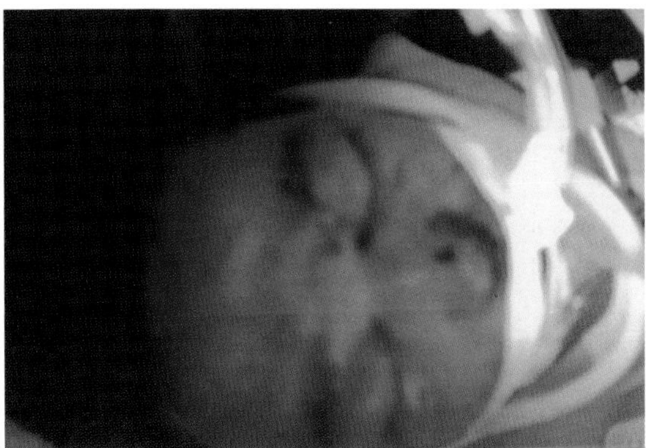

was grabbing for a knife, so he tackled him. And the fight was over so quickly, they couldn't have done that much damage.

Thursday, April 13, 2000

Four days later, doctors finally operated on Mark's eye. His face was "peeled back and...the bone fragments were removed. The eye floor was rebuilt with a prosthesis."

The prosthesis was essentially a plastic cup, inserted behind his eyeball to keep it from sinking into his head. To this day, Mark can feel the cup's seam under his skin. Aside from the feeling of the prosthesis, all other physical traces of the attack were erased by Mark's plastic surgeon.

Monday, April 17, 2000

After nine days in a coma, Mark finally came around. Now the real evaluation would begin. Doctors had seen some volume loss in Mark's brain, but the extent of brain damage could only really be assessed by comparing a person's current abilities to their abilities before the trauma.

It wasn't good.

At first, Mark couldn't speak at all. After a few days, he began to form words, but it was clear he had amnesia. He thought it was 1984 and that he was in a naval hospital.

"I remember opening up my eyes and seeing that asbestos ceiling design, and I didn't know where I was," Mark recalled. "I thought that I was in a naval hospital in Spain. I mean, that's how far back these guys knocked me."

A police photo of Mark in the hospital after the attack.
(photo provided by the Ulster County Sheriff's Office)

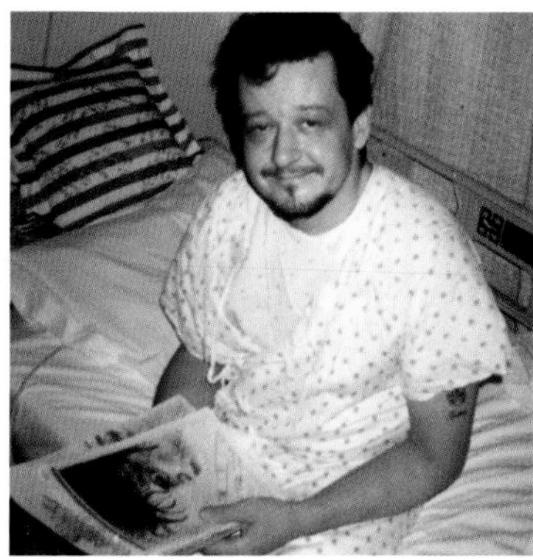

Mark found he could remember his immediate family but no one else from his recent past—not even his young niece or nephew. He'd lost most of his adult memories—his alcoholic past, his former marriage, friendships. And he'd forgotten how to do simple everyday things, like tying his shoes, going to the bathroom, or eating with a fork.

The damage to Mark's brain caused other issues as well. He had to learn how to walk again. His depth perception was off. And his right hand—his drawing hand—shook badly.

While Mark took his literal first steps toward recovery, his friend and Anchorage coworker, Tom, began to prepare for Mark's eventual release from the hospital. Before the attack, Mark and Tom had made arrangements to move in together to save on expenses. Now Tom found himself in the unanticipated position of being Mark's principal caregiver and closest friend.

Tom worked for weeks to get permission from the housing authority to enter and clean Mark's apartment, where open containers of food had spoiled. "They only let me in there like a day before he came home from the hospital. I wasn't aware of the amount that he drank. I found about fifty half-gallon liquor bottles in his apartment—under the bed, in the closets, piles of them. I cleaned all of that out."

After forty-three days in the hospital, Mark's Medicaid ran out. He was discharged and sent home with Tom, who took him back to an apartment and a life he didn't remember.

Mark in the hospital after surgery.

opposite: The first entry in Mark's recovery journal.

JUNE 8, 2000

I GOT OUT OF THE HOSPITAL ON THE 17TH OF MAY.

I WAS BEAT UP BY FIVE GUYS ON THE 7TH OF APRIL.

I CAN'T EVAN WRITE MY NAME

I HAVE TO LEARN ALL OVER AGAIN.

Mark E. Hogancamp

6.14.00

I'm sitting here alone waiting for Tom to get finished with work.

I am practising my guitar right now, and I'm not that bad at it.

This is how I write now. My right hand still wants to shake.

signed/;

Mark E. Hogancamp

THE ONE
WHO STARTED
IT ALL.!!

CHAPTER THREE

The Trials

"I had to testify three times. Three times I had to see those guys. And one of them was looking at his nails in the courtroom like, 'Come on...this is a hassle.' // I remember the prosecutor opened up a folder with four photographs of my injuries, but he wouldn't show them to me because he didn't know how they would affect me. // Then he asked me in front of the whole jury, 'Mark, are you gay? Are you homosexual?' And I said no. They said, 'Are you a cross-dresser?' And I said yeah. // A woman from crime victims was in the courtroom when I was going through the trials. She gave me this little teddy bear, so I could hold it under the witness stand and channel my feelings into it instead of on my face. And that thing was so sweaty and smashed by the end from me squeezing it so tight, she had to give me another one."

opposite: A Nazi prepped for a public hanging.

July 31, 2001

Your Honor:

There is a need in me to express my feelings and the impact the assault of these five people had on my son's life and also on the family.

Do they know how a mother feels to receive a call 6:00 a.m. on a Saturday morning that her son has been found on the street and has been admitted to the Hospital with severe head injuries, the extent not quite known yet, but he is placed on life support and will be transported to Westchester Medical Center, which is better equipped to treat his injuries. Do they know what agony it was to see your son that day and almost not recognizing him? Seeing him day after day still on the life support system, not knowing if he realizes anything around him or recognizing anybody? Ten days later most tubes are disconnected from his body and the joy of all of us to witness him responding. Then the heartbreaking time starts. To see your son at 38 years old not being able to feed himself, not recognizing most family members, able to talk only in a strained whisper and limited vocabulary? Never realizing watching him take his first steps at one year old to have to witness him at 38 years old take those first wobbling steps again, and again being overjoyed and happy to watch the progress. After 40 days he finally is discharged from the hospital with many, many months of various therapies ahead of him. He was not able to be on his own and needed a roommate to help with every day ordinary tasks. He was fearful to leave the apartment alone. He still, to this day, is very apprehensive to be too far away from home on his own. After 15 months since the assault, he is still struggling to cope. We still do not know if his fine motor skills or creativity will ever be completely restored. To watch his extreme frustrations not able to do things he was able to prior the assault is very painful for all of us. He feels "imprisoned" with his own inabilities to function properly.

What I do not understand is how anybody can intentionally harm another person to this extent and have no apparent remorse or conscious. I wonder if they ever would treat a dog this way. I feel all five men were involved and part of this horrendous crime. It does not matter now, after they have been apprehended, who only kicked a "little" or a "lot". The fact remains they all were present and no one seemed to feel at any time later that maybe they should get some help for Mark. He was left to die. They did not care what would happen to him. "An eye for an eye" is not acceptable by law, but the maximum prison term for such a crime should be. At the least they would experience how it feels to be "imprisoned".

Respectfully,

Edda Eller

Edda (Hogancamp) Eller

While Mark was rebuilding his life, detectives were building a case against his five attackers. The prosecution was led by Emmanuel Nneji, the then assistant district attorney for Ulster County.

In his first life, Mark might have overlooked Nneji, a colossus of a man who emigrated from Nigeria in 1980. But in his second life, Mark appreciated Nneji's kindness, his sharp sense of justice, and his dogged pursuit of the facts.

Nneji suspected that Mark's attack may have been a hate crime. The bartender, and even some of the attackers, had overheard Mark telling Freddy Hommel that he was a cross-dresser, and all had noted Hommel's discomfort. But Nneji couldn't find enough evidence to support a hate-crime conviction, so he and detectives followed a different route.

Records show that four months before the attack, Richard Purcell, David Mead, Noah Rand, and Black Freddy signed an oath to the local branch of a national prison gang. The affiliation was enough to get the attackers charged with gang assault.

In May of 2000, the five attackers were indicted by an Ulster County grand jury for gang assault in the first and second degree, and reckless endangerment in the first degree. The heat of a fight may turn men into brothers, but when prison is on the line, those bonds can evaporate in an instant. It was every man for himself.

Rand claimed he hadn't touched Mark, but he had failed to report the attack and he had driven one of the cars that sped away from the scene. Rather than face a jury, he decided to plead guilty to lesser charges: assault in the third degree and reckless endangerment in the first degree. He received a sentence of five years' probation.

Like Rand, Mead claimed he hadn't hurt Mark. But detectives reported that Mead had initially told them a phony story and had hidden and replaced his shoes from the night of the attack. Nevertheless, Mead's family fought the charges with a vengeance.

His lawyer submitted one character letter after another, each describing Mead as a good kid who'd been in the wrong place at the wrong time. He ultimately proceeded to trial and was acquitted of everything except assault in the third degree and reckless endangerment in the first degree. He received the same sentence as Rand: five years' probation.

Black Freddy was a more challenging case. He'd lied to the police at first but ultimately admitted to kicking Mark as much as any of his fellow attackers. He had a troubling history of violence and substance abuse, but

opposite: A letter to the judge from Mark's mother.

he was from a broken home and had suffered from depression. He had also been a minor at the time of the attack and claimed that he had only joined in so he wouldn't be an outcast.

Black Freddy ultimately pled guilty to all charges and cooperated with authorities, even testifying at the trials of his fellow attackers. In return, he received the minimum sentence of five years in prison.

Hommel, the undisputed instigator of the attack, quickly agreed to a plea deal. He testified that he had initiated the fight but hadn't hurt Mark—the damage, he claimed, had been done by Purcell.

"Richie was jumping on his head with both feet together...jumping on the guy's head and his chest," he said in court. In the end, Hommel received a reduced five-year prison sentence.

So it all came down to Purcell. He hadn't started the fight, but witnesses raised disturbing details during his trial. Purcell was allegedly the one who had convinced Mead, Rand, and Black Freddy to join the gang and had fought someone on Hommel's behalf before. After he stomped on Mark's head with his heavy boots, the other attackers remembered having to "pull [Purcell] away from the victim to get him to stop." He had shown off the blood on his boots to his friend Steve. And the others claimed he had tried

above and opposite: The SS in Marwencol were inspired by Mark's five attackers. They are immortal killing machines, perpetually terrorizing Marwencol in their hunt for Mark's alter ego, Hogie.

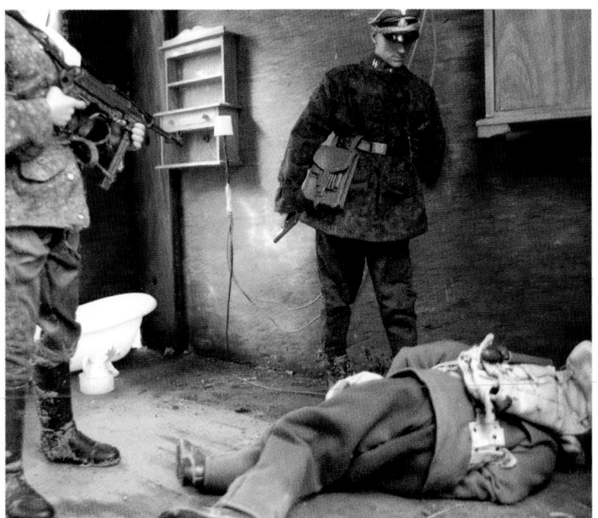

to convince Black Freddy to take the blame for the attack since Black Freddy was a minor and would ostensibly get into the least amount of trouble.

After one mistrial, Purcell pled guilty and received a sentence of nine years in prison. While his sentence was sixteen years below the twenty-five-year maximum, Purcell's attorney tried to appeal its severity. The appeal was denied.

Years later, Mark's attackers became the inspiration for the band of five deadly SS soldiers who terrorize Marwencol. Mark eventually shared some of his Marwencol stories and photos with Nneji, who said Mark's art touched him very significantly. "If somebody is in pain, you can see it in his art. It's nice that, if somebody hurts you, you can—without any violence—get back at them."

The attackers were also featured in the documentary *Marwencol* by director Jeff Malmberg; however, the director chose not to reveal the fates of the five attackers. "Every time I tried to include the information about the trials, it gave Mark's story a false sense of closure, as if justice had been served. It certainly never felt that way to Mark—he never felt any sense of resolution—so I didn't feel it was fair to give that to the audience."

By 2010 all five of Mark's attackers were free and living dual lives as regular citizens in the real world and SS soldiers in Marwencol.

OFFICIAL

CHAPTER FOUR

Recovery

"I used to have a photographic memory, and my imagination was vivid...like there were color movies going on in my head. But when I woke up after the attack, there was nothing. It was jumbled, all over the place. // My father brought some drawings of mine to the hospital; he thought maybe they would spark up some memories. I knew I could draw, and I tried to, but I can't draw the way I used to anymore. // I wanted to bring it back—my imagination—because I knew my mind was an eight-cylinder engine that's only running on one cylinder. So I figured to get it back, I would build my own bar. Because I always wanted my own place. So I built it...and then it looked weird all by itself out there, so I built other buildings to keep it company. // I was so proud of what I was doing. I was so proud of my accomplishments, and that my imagination was coming back, that I wanted to share it with people."

opposite: Mark working in Marwencol in 2005. (photo by Tom Putnam)

November

I really love you...

Maria

11/93

I'm really freaked
I'm gonna die tonight...

January 19, 1993

Last entry...

After settling into his new apartment, Mark threw himself into therapy. He was gradually improving when his state-supported physical, occupational, and cognitive therapies ran out less than a year after the attack. He was thirty-eight, broke, disabled, and angry. He realized he had two choices: he could give up and "let those five guys win," or he could take control of his own recovery.

He started by paging through his "drunk journals" in an effort to recall his past. The picture he pieced together wasn't pretty. The alcoholism. The divorce. The jail time. The string of failures and disappointments.

For most people, reliving such dark memories would be a crushing experience. But for Mark, it was as if someone else had written the diaries—someone with a past and an addiction that he didn't have. He had a clean slate, so he set about selecting which parts of his first life would stay and which would go.

"Racism, prejudice, hatred, addiction...I figure those were learned things, so I could unlearn them in my second life."

First on the chopping block was his alcoholism. After forty-three days in the hospital, he wasn't physically dependent on liquor. He couldn't even remember what it tasted or smelled like, but he saw how destructive it could be. He vowed to never touch it again. Instead, he changed his drink of choice to coffee. Pots and pots of coffee.

The attack also wiped out his memories of cross-dressing. When Tom first brought him back to the apartment, Mark spotted his shoe collection and assumed it belonged to a girlfriend.

After reading his diaries, he realized that cross-dressing had brought him pleasure in his first life and hadn't hurt him or anyone else. So he slipped his foot into a high-heeled shoe and was immediately hit with a sense memory. In a flash, his love of women's shoes was back. And it proved an unexpected boon to his recovery.

"I put on heels to get my balance back," Mark recalled. "A lot of falling down and broken heels later, I got my balance to where I could walk across the street and not trip or fall."

Once he made it across the street, Mark found something else that interested him: women. Namely, an Anchorage waitress named Wendy with spiky "Pat Benatar hair" and a tall, blonde neighbor named Colleen. Unfortunately, both Wendy and Colleen were married, but they played important roles as supportive friends and Mark's first second-life crushes.

opposite: A page from Mark's "drunk journal."

Two years after the attack, Tom needed to move to Seattle to care for his ailing mother. Mark couldn't afford the rent on his own, so his mother moved him into a trailer in a rural outskirt of Kingston. Mark had his independence back, but he was lonely.

Television helped to a point. It replenished his cultural references and showed him how to interact with people. But the real turning point came when he rediscovered his interest in World War II and military miniatures.

His right hand shook too much to paint the small models he'd worked on before his attack, so Janet and Mark Wikane of J&J's Hobbies suggested he try the twelve-inch, 1:6 scale figures.

He found one that looked a bit like him—"Tom," a US 82nd Airborne Pathfinder by Dragon Models Limited—and called him Captain Hogancamp, or "Hogie" for short.

Dressing his 1:6 scale figure turned out to be much more challenging than Mark expected. The clothing was small and difficult to pull on, but the process ultimately helped him improve his dexterity and patience.

Over time, Mark picked up other figures that resembled his friends: Barbies for Colleen and Wendy, action figures for his Anchorage friends

Mark in the Church Hill Road apartment he shared with Tom Neubauer after the attack.

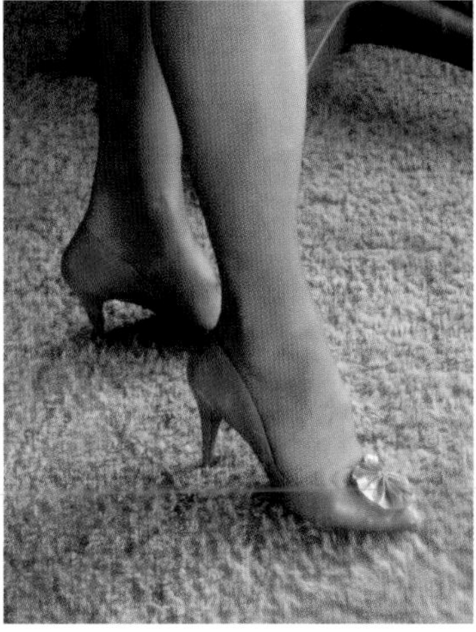
A.

B.

and brothers, and a James Bond Pussy Galore figure that was the spitting image of his mother.

"Most of my dolls have a character from a real person," Mark explains. "Like my brother the cop. My father came up and saw Gregg's figure on a shelf and he said, 'Hey, that looks like your brother.' Well, that's because it is."

Soon Mark had a collection of figures with very real personalities but no place to congregate. So he found some scrap plywood and screwed it together into the shape of a small building—a tavern—which he put behind his trailer.

He named the bar Hogancamp's Ruined Stocking Catfight Club. It was the business he'd always dreamed of owning—a cozy, cluttered tavern that offered entertainment in the form of staged catfights between the ladies.

From the beginning, Mark set his bar and its patrons in World War II. His early fascination with the period endured, even after his attack. In his mind, it was a romantic era when men were brave and women were feminine, yet strong.

After he finished the bar, he decided to erect buildings for the town's other two "founders." For Wendy, he built a cafe called Wendy Lee's Kitchen;

A. A self-portrait of Mark in heels after his attack.
B. Mark's mother with her alter ego.

for Colleen, a shop called Pocket Full of Posies. Even the budding town's name honors his friends: Marwencol is a combination of the three founders' names.

Soon the characters in Marwencol began to inspire stories in Mark's mind. During visits to the Anchorage, Mark told his friends about their exciting second lives, but they didn't believe him. So he found his old point-and-shoot 35 mm Pentax camera from college and started photographing the dramas as proof.

His earliest photos were often over- or underexposed or shot from unnatural angles (e.g., the top two photos on the facing page). But his lens soon caught up with his imagination.

Mark's friends loved his photos so much that he worked up the courage to send some shots to a 1:6 scale fan page called the Ultimate Soldier. The photos were enthusiastically received, and Mark inherited a new virtual community. Some of his fellow club members even sent Mark their own 1:6 scale alter egos, who became characters in Marwencol.

Shortly after Mark joined the Ultimate Soldier website, he entered its 1:6 scale photo contest with a shot entitled *Rescuing the Major* (page 58), which depicts his brother Mike carrying a wounded army major during a *Waffen-SS* ambush. The photo is so realistic, it's often mistaken for an actual photo from World War II.

Mark won the contest and earned enough prize money to buy a Dragon Models Limited figure named Anna, who became the love interest for his alter ego. Shortly thereafter, Mark acquired a third figure to create a romantic triangle—a Blue Box International Cy Girl named Alaqua, whom he renamed Deja Thoris, the Belgian Witch of Marwencol.

The stage was set for an epic drama, and stories began to flood into Mark's mind. Suddenly, he didn't feel so alone in his trailer. "Because everything is so far away from me, I figured I'd bring the world to me," Mark said. "So here's my little world, where I can make things happen... and I can create anything I want."

What he'd created was a customized form of therapy that would help him recover from his emotional and physical wounds, and forever change the course of his life.

"Those guys don't know what they took from me. I figured I'll never get all those memories back, so I'll just make new ones."

opposite: Early 35 mm "shoebox" images from the inception of Marwencol, ca. 2004–05.

20321727
WENDY LEE'S KITCHEN
"THE LOSERS"
OPEN

Rescuing the Major—the 2004 photo that won the Ultimate Soldier contest.

Patton and the Jeep—another of Mark's earliest 35 mm Marwencol photos, ca. 2004.

CHAPTER FIVE

Discovery

"I went from having nobody around to creating my own town so I could be in control of something, because I didn't have control of anything else in my life. And now other people want to be a part of it. // It's a weird experience having people document me documenting my life. Answering questions...talking to people. But I decided I'm not going to lie in my second life. I always tell the truth and tell people who I am, because why should I be afraid to tell you who I am? // That's exactly the message that I want to send to people—just be yourself. The longer I live life in this world that humans created, the more I'm finding out people don't accept everything that other people have to offer. There's prejudice... that's a trait that we learn from other humans. // So I'm glad if my will to fight has given others hope. It's good hearing from people who've been helped by my story...by my town. That's why I did all this—the art show, the documentary, the book. 'For duty and humanity.'"

opposite: Mark wearing down his jeep's tires in 2009.
(photo by Chris Shellen)

n April 8, 2000,

A.

B.

C.

A. A spread from *Esopus* magazine's piece on Marwencol. (courtesy of *Esopus* magazine)

B. Mark at White Columns Gallery in 2006. (photo by Tom Putnam)

C. Mark working with director Jeff Malmberg on the documentary *Marwencol* in 2008. (photo by Chris Shellen)

In the winter of 2005, photographer David Naugle was living in Kingston with his wife. One day, the pair spotted a curious sight: a man in a World War II uniform slowly pedaling his bicycle through three inches of snow.

Several months later, David saw the man again, this time pulling a small jeep full of dolls along the road. David finally worked up the courage to introduce himself, and Mark rewarded David's curiosity with an envelope full of early photos of life in Marwencol.

The photos were incredible—unlike anything David had ever seen. He shared them with his friend Tod Lippy, editor of *Esopus* magazine, a celebrated nonprofit arts journal. With Mark's blessing, the two collaborated on a piece about Marwencol in the fall 2005 issue of *Esopus*.

The piece attracted the attention of filmmaker Jeff Malmberg, who contacted Mark about shooting a documentary on Marwencol. Around the same time, Lippy showed Mark's work to a curator at Manhattan's White Columns, who suggested staging a show of Mark's work as a part of the gallery's *Other People's Projects* series.

A public showing of his private therapy in New York City presented an intensely difficult decision for Mark, who rarely left the security of his trailer. In the end, Mark decided to make his story public with the hope that it might help other people. The White Columns show opened in May 2006 and was popular with both critics and visitors.

Four years later, Malmberg's feature documentary *Marwencol* premiered at Austin's South by Southwest (SXSW) Film Festival, where it won the Grand Jury Prize for Best Documentary. It went on to win more than twenty-five international awards, including two Independent Spirit Awards and Best Documentary of the Year from the Boston Society of Film Critics.

In 2010 the film had its theatrical premiere at New York's IFC Center. Mark attended the premiere alongside Naugle, Lippy, and Malmberg.

Mark staged a miniature "red carpet" premiere in front of the theater with the film's leading ladies. After the show, he participated in a Q&A with Naugle, Lippy, and Malmberg. When Mark revealed to the audience that he'd worn high heels to the premiere, he received a thunderous standing ovation.

After the release of the documentary and a short segment on the Emmy Award–winning Showtime series *This American Life*, Mark's life began to change significantly.

Some changes were difficult. His mother passed away shortly before the documentary's premiere. Later on, a few well-meaning fans found out

A.

B.

where Mark lived and showed up on his doorstep hoping to talk to him. But other changes were more positive.

Once ridiculed as "the guy who plays with dolls," Mark became respected as an artist by local residents, who encouraged him to wear heels in public. He was approached by Kingston's One Mile Gallery to represent his art. People from around the world donated figures, vehicles, and props to his town, along with letters of support and thanks for sharing his story. And perhaps most importantly, his therapeutic outlet was legitimized and celebrated, giving his time spent in Marwencol a sense of purpose.

Today, he feels less afraid when he ventures into town, but he still prefers the safety of his home and the small town that lives just outside of its doors. With some of his dexterity returned, Mark is experimenting with even smaller figures through a series of World War II–themed dioramas. But he continues to document the daily adventures in the town of Marwencol.

"The day I die…that's when my story ends."

A. Mark's 1:6 scale "red carpet" premiere in front of Manhattan's IFC Center in 2010.

B. Mark and well-wishers following a screening of the documentary. (photo by Matt Radecki)

"A photographer takes a photo of Anna and me at Marwencol Falls, where we spent our honeymoon."

C

Hogie draws Anna's portrait for her in his diary.

American GIs look at a map on the hood of their jeep during the bitter Belgian winter of 1944.

Part II

INSIDE MARWENCOL

DR. F. SHIMKETS, MD.

CHAPTER SIX

Process

"When I set up or shoot a scene, it's as if the characters tell me what to do. It's like they don't even hear me...they just do what they want. // Each figure has a personality—even the characters that aren't based on any one person in the real world, like Deja Thoris. So, with my camera, I'm trying to take something plastic and make it look real, because in my head it's real. I see it as real, but nobody else around me does. // When it gets cold, I put coats on my figures, because that's what I would do in real life. And I know how an American World War II soldier's coat feels and moves because I have one. Does it keep me warm in the winter? No, not really...so I understand why some people froze in the Ardennes forest. // Even the ambient noises make it more real. I come out here and I hear the train whistling and the gunfire from the gun range that's a mile away and it all adds to the story in my head. It's like I'm trying to capture the whole story in one photograph, because it's not a moving picture—they're more like stills from a movie. I'm trying to capture that mood...that moment when you can almost smell the grass or the rain and feel the rocks or the mud or the snow."

opposite: Mark at work in Marwencol. (photo by Jeff Malmberg)

Plans for the Marwencol Theatre (which later became Marwencol Town Hall) and Malmberg Film Studios.

A.

B.

Constructing Marwencol

Mark built Marwencol entirely by hand—a painstakingly long process that began in 2002 with the construction of Hogancamp's Ruined Stocking Catfight Club. The design for the bar and subsequent buildings came from Mark's imagination and spotty memories of his days building trade-show sets. He sketched basic plans and foraged for building materials on roadsides and in trash heaps.

Each building is an artfully assembled patchwork of found wood, windows, roof shingles, nails, and screws. And each is inspired by something specific: a person (Wendy Lee's Kitchen, Pocket Full of Posies), a place (the Anchorage), a dream (Hogancamp's bar), a loss (the Federal Cancer Center), a memory (the Marlo Inn), or an event (the great flood in the Kingston area in 2005 that resulted in the Church of Marwencol).

To make shooting photos of scenes inside the structures easier, Mark equipped them with clever forms of access—a window in place of a roof, a removable false front, or, in the case of the Town Hall, enough empty space for Mark to sit inside the building to shoot on rainy days.

Mark outfitted each of his structures with small props and furniture that were either found, donated by friends, or made by hand. Broken windshield glass along the roadside became ice in the drinks at Hogancamp's. Hogie's coffee cup held real coffee. Old photos and small images in magazines were used as wall art. Sofas were constructed by attaching cotton and fabric remnants to bricks.

He arranged the buildings in two parallel rows, forming a main street down the center of town, and ran his vehicles back and forth to create realistic tire tracks in the mud. Then he completed the illusion with small plants, flowers, and moss around the perimeter of his town—anything that looked authentic in miniature.

A. Marwencol Town Hall and Malmberg Film Studios under construction.

B. Mark inside the Town Hall. The removable glass roof, made of reclaimed windows, enables him to shoot from inside on rainy days. On clear days, Mark can shoot through the roof as well as the building's front doors and removable walls.

above: Mark's budding town after four years of work. (photo by Tom Putnam)
bottom: The town in the back of his new trailer in 2011. (photo by Jeff Malmberg)

opposite: Marwencol expanded to include a Nazi encampment in front of Mark's trailer. (photo by Jeff Malmberg)

"When I grab my camera and go outside, I don't get the feeling that the town is moving or alive until I lie down in the mud or stones, and I'm at their level. It's such a different perspective. When I'm photographing from that angle, I'm their height and it looks like somebody their size took it."

Photographing Marwencol

Having taken only a few photos in his life, Mark's early photographic process moved at a glacial pace. The light meter on his camera was broken, so he would set up his figures, shoot a series of photos, mail the spent rolls to a film lab for processing, and wait a few weeks for the prints. If the photos were poorly exposed or the angle wasn't right, he would reshoot the story from the beginning.

A few years after creating Marwencol, Mark's beat-up old Pentax finally died. To help him continue his therapy, Mark's mother bought him a digital camera—a Canon G6.

"She bought me a brand new Canon 7.1 megapixel digital camera, and I went from using a 35 mm, which was simple and manual, to this thing, which I hated, because I didn't understand it."

On New Year's Eve 2005, desperate to film his bar's festivities, Mark finally shut out all distractions and sat down with the camera's manual.

"I didn't want to know about all the fancy doodads. I just wanted to record my New Year's Eve party. So I did, and the shots came out perfect."

Mark's new digital camera turned out to be much better than just a replacement. The camera's flip-out viewer freed him from having to look through the viewfinder and enabled him to fit the camera into the tiny spaces occupied by his characters. And he was no longer restricted to twenty-four images every few weeks. With instant feedback and unlimited room to experiment, Mark was suddenly free to shoot as much as he wanted, whenever he wanted. He could experiment with different lighting schemes and new angles and setups.

He lay down on his stomach in the dirt, mud, and snow, bugs crawling all over him, in order to put his lens at eye level with his figures. He shot large tableaus, close-ups, over-the-shoulder shots, and reverse shots—just like in the movies—so his stories would feel more cinematic. At last, his photos reflected the rich adventures he saw in his mind.

The Losers jeep, fully weathered in 2010.

A.

B.

C.

"Factory tires always have a seam running down the center of the tire. So now...I could sand the seams off, but where is the realism in that? // The first thing I bought was a Scout car, and I was like, damn, the tires they look so brand new, they've got a little factory seam around every one, it looks like it just rolled off a showroom. I don't want that...so I started dragging stuff. // If I don't have the jeep packed with dolls, I fill it up with rocks. I'll put those in there to add weight and so it makes tire tracks while I'm wearing down the tires. The jeep has 180 miles on it, which is 1,080 miles in 1:6 scale, so I'm getting close to as many miles as the jeep would have run in actuality. // To other people it's crazy, but to me it's a purpose, to wear down the tires and make things look real so there isn't a factory-shiny plastic seam on them. In war, things aren't clean like that."

A. The jeep attached to a pool cue for towing.
B. The jeep "parked" at Mark's local store in 2010.
C. The jeep being pulled behind Mark's bicycle.

To increase the realism of his figures' uniforms, Mark ages them by leaving them out in the dirt, mud, rain, or snow until they look authentic.

When a character needs to be asleep or deceased, Mark "closes" their eyes with flesh-colored Sculpey clay and paint.

Flesh wounds are made by heating the figure with a lighter and pressing a pen through the skin, mimicking a bullet's trajectory by lifting up or pushing down.

Blood is either red-colored sugar water ("the ants love it") or nail polish, which looks wet and fresh for months, giving Mark more time to shoot.

Every briefcase, satchel, and bag is filled with real items that belong to the figure, such as guns, ammo, documents, money, smokes, and magazines.

To make realistic bullet holes, Mark heats up the end of a metal pen and presses it through the body of a vehicle or the plastic windshield.

Mark uses Christmas and dollhouse lights to illuminate his town after dark.

To authentically weather his vehicles, Mark paints around each vehicle's seams and grommets with steel model paint.

The natural environment of Kingston is incorporated into Mark's photos, with faraway vistas looking size appropriate.

By watching TV after his attack, Mark learned to think cinematically. He shoots over-the-shoulder, close-up, and grand establishing shots.

To help his figures stand, Mark sometimes buries their feet in soft dirt or snow...

...or props them up from behind with metal or wooden stakes planted in the ground.

ATTENTION!
PEOPLE OF
DEADWOOD
$7,000 IN GOLD
REWARD OF $2500
$1200 TO THE CAPTURE
$1300 FOR THE RECOVERY
L.F. ROWELL
Dear Sally,
The fighting today was a
harsh we nearly lost half of our
command and the captain took
a shot to the left arm. I think
they had to remove it. I hope
everything back at home is good
with you and ma. Make sure no
With Love,
Your brother Jeb
P.S. Tell ma to keep eattin

Neighboring towns are named after actual towns in Belgium (usually World War II sites) or fictional 1:6 scale towns created by Mark's friends in the club.

opposite: Plastic jewelry/craft cases from Goodwill hold Mark's collection of spare hands, props, documents, shoes, and various foraged materials.

Scott Merry apprehends German flying ace
Von Arnold after shooting him out of the sky.

MARWENCO

CHAPTER SEVEN

The Town

"After it was done, I stood back and thought, wow, it's a town, with my bar, Colleen's shop, and Wendy's place...but it doesn't have a name. // And then I thought, I like the way Belgium sounds. A lot happened in Belgium during the war, so I figure, all right, I'll put the town in Belgium. But what should I call it? And I tried to think—Schmedlyville, Markville, Hogesville, Hogestown, Mark's Town, Doll Town, Weeble Town. Then I figured, hey, there're three of us that have buildings in the town, why not combine our names? // It took me a week and a half of switching 'Colleen,' 'Wendy,' and 'Mark' around—Colwenmar, Wencolmar, Marcolwen—until I came up with Marwencol: 'Mark,' 'Wendy,' 'Colleen.' And that's the town's name. That's when I built the water tower. I had an old coffee can—a big coffee can—and put the name on it. // The name Marwencol doesn't have the same significance it had when I first created the town and gave it that name. Those two women, they're so distant from my life right now, but that's the whole reason for me naming it Marwencol... because those two women were my first crushes coming out of the brain injury."

opposite: Marwencol's first water tower, in 2006.

Main Street, Marwencol

(photo by Jeff Malmberg)

A. **Marwencol Town Hall**
Built: 2008
Marwencol's meeting hall

B. **Malmberg Film Studios**
Built: 2008
Second-floor film studio of director Jeff Malmberg

C. **Guard Shack and Gate**
Built: 2007
Security post at the entrance of Marwencol

D. **Mr. Magic's Ice Cream Fountain**
Built: 2010
Unfinished home of Tom's ice cream parlor

E. **Dr. F. Shimkets**
Built: 2007
Two-story medical facility

F. **The Bank of Marwencol**
Built: 2008
Official financial institution of Marwencol

G. **Stoffel-Navarro Park**
Dedicated: 2009
Marwencol's main town park

H. **Tonjes's Furniture**
Built: 2007
Tonjes's furniture workshop and apartment

I. **Hogancamp's Red Ball Express**
Built: 2007
Vehicle-repair shop

J. **Marwencol's Gas Station**
Built: 2006
Refueling station for Marwencol's vehicles

K. **Federal Cancer Research**
Built: 2002
Second-floor research center

L. **The Anchorage**
Built: 2002
Marwencol's popular dinner spot

M. **Marlo Inn**
Built: 2006
Marwencol's Main Street inn

N. **Marwencol Cemetery**
Built: 2002
Marwencol's official town cemetery

O. **The Church of Marwencol**
Built: 2005
Marwencol's church and memorial to the flood of 2005

not shown:
Hogancamp's Ruined Stocking Catfight Club
Nazi Headquarters

Hogancamp's Ruined Stocking Catfight Club

Hogancamp's was Marwencol's first building. Initially on the main street of town, the bar was moved indoors to allow Mark to continue shooting in inclement weather. It was later expanded to include a second-floor apartment and barracks. The bar is named for its featured entertainment: staged female catfights. Almost everything in the bar represents something sentimental to Mark, from the vintage photo of his father to his American flag patch.

The Anchorage

The Anchorage is a 1:6 scale version of the Kingston restaurant where Mark worked before the attack. In the early days of Marwencol, the Anchorage was housed in a smaller one-story building. Later it moved to the ground floor of the former Wendy Lee's Kitchen. Like its brick-and-mortar counterpart, the Anchorage is owned and run by Julie Swarthout (or rather, her 1:6 scale alter ego).

Marlo Inn

To support the growing number of visitors to Marwencol, Mark added the Marlo Inn, a 1:6 scale replica of Mark's first workplace. The Marlo Inn is home to one of Marwencol's three town bars and is known as one of the more dangerous places in town. It's wired with working lights and music speakers.

A patron in front of Hogancamp's Ruined Stocking Catfight Club in its original setting outdoors.

Hogie showing Anna the new Marwencol Town Hall.

Marwencol Town Hall

By 2008 Mark had acquired enough figures that he was in need of a central meeting hall. He drew up plans for a two-story town hall—large enough that Mark himself could sit inside it on rainy days to shoot photos. The town hall was designed to host cultural events, including concerts and movies. It also features a removable roof made from a window, through which Mark can photograph or use as a covering for rainy-day photo shoots.

Malmberg Film Studios

To assist director Jeff Malmberg in finishing the documentary *Marwencol*, Mark constructed an apartment/film studio on the second floor of Marwencol's new town hall. Jeff shares the carpeted apartment with his wife, Chris Shellen. The couple uses it as a film studio and salon for hosting small gatherings of Marwencol residents.

The Church of Marwencol

In 2005 a spring storm flooded Kingston, destroying Mark's trailer and many of his neighbors' homes. After Mark's mother moved him into a new trailer, he gathered a piece of wood from every flooded house. With the help of Marwencol's townspeople, he constructed the Church of Marwencol to commemorate the flood and honor those who had lost their homes. Engineered with five possible photographic angles, the church includes a bell tower to warn of impending floods. The Church of Marwencol is presided over by Father Raymond Bradbury.

The Church of Marwencol in the snow.

Townspeople building the church out of wood salvaged from homes destroyed in the flood of 2005.

The Bank of Marwencol

The Bank of Marwencol is the town's official financial center. Deja Thoris acts as the bank's manager, with a rotating staff of Marwencol ladies working behind the counter. The bank's roof is constructed of a removable window, which protects it from rain and snow. The floor is covered with a carpet remnant, and the wallpaper is leftover contact paper. In the back sits a hidden vault, which contains all of Marwencol's money and jewels.

Stoffel-Navarro Park

Stoffel-Navarro Park is a small town park dedicated to the late John Stoffel and his wife, Liz Navarro, owners of the former Atlantic Toys, from which Mark purchased the Anna figure. The park features a baby pine tree and several plants chosen for their small leaves. Standing above the plants is a platform that serves as a lookout/sniper post and popular sunbathing spot. It's also home to the Marwencol water tower.

Mr. Magic's Ice Cream Fountain

In 2009 Mark broke ground on a new building on Main Street, set to become Mr. Magic's Ice Cream Fountain—an ice cream parlor run by Mark's former roommate, Tom. Construction has been slow. As of the printing of this book, the building has yet to be completed.

Deja Thoris enters the Bank of Marwencol
to deposit a priceless jewel.

Deja and Dr. Schneider sunbathe on the platform above Stoffel-Navarro Park.

STO

Federal Cancer Research

Above the Anchorage is a space that has changed hands several times. In the early days of Marwencol, it was home to Pocket Full of Posies, a boutique owned by Mark's neighbor Colleen. When Colleen moved away, Pocket Full of Posies closed and was briefly the site of a brothel. When the mother of Mark's friend Bert died from cancer, Mark dedicated the top floor of the building to cancer research and renamed it the Federal Cancer Research.

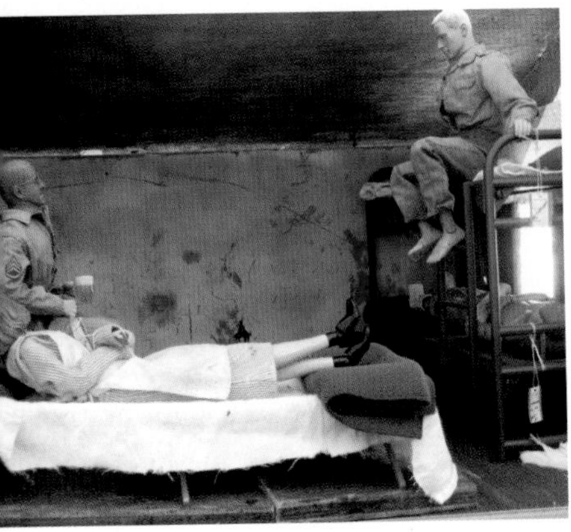

Dr. F. Shimkets

Dr. F. Shimkets's office is a two-story medical building housing a doctor's office on the ground floor and an infirmary on the second floor. The building is named after the town's doctor—Dr. F. Shimkets, also known as Medi-Jeep. Many soldiers have recuperated in the infirmary upstairs, which is staffed by a volunteer corps of nurses that includes Mark's mother (shown resting on the bed).

Marwencol Cemetery

Marwencol's cemetery is home to the grave of Mark's beloved pet bird, Baby, who died in 2006, as well as other Marwencol figures. After the flood of 2005, which destroyed Mark's trailer, the cemetery was relocated to the new site of Marwencol. There, the bodies were reburied in the tradition of World War II funerals.

Allied soldiers pull water up to POWs being held in the cancer center.

A soldier pays his respects to his buddy in Marwencol's cemetery.

Lt. Tonjes at the public unveiling of his statue, *Satan's Defeat*.

Lt. Tonjes takes a break from sweeping Marwencol's gas station to talk with Mailman.

Hogancamp's Red Ball Express

In order to service Marwencol's growing fleet of motorcycles, jeeps, *Kübelwagens*, tanks, and planes, Mark built Hogancamp's Red Ball Express, a 1:6 scale version of a car repair shop at which Mark's grandfather once worked. The Red Ball Express is staffed by both of Mark's grandfathers—German Grandpa Ewald and Polish Grandpa Hogancamp. It features working lights for late-night jobs and a store of vehicle spare parts.

Marwencol's Gas Station

Before Marwencol welcomed Hogancamp's Red Ball Express, residents took their vehicles to the town gas station. Open day and night, the gas station features working shop and pump lights. The gas pump is elevated above the street to facilitate service to larger war vehicles, such as tanks and Kübelwagens.

Tonjes's Furniture

Lt. Tonjes is the 1:6 scale alter ego of one of Mark's friends from the Ultimate Soldier fan site. Tonjes started out as a chaplain in Marwencol's church. After performing Anna and Hogie's second wedding ceremony, he resigned the priesthood to become a carpenter. He lives and works in the small Tonjes's Furniture shop in the Red Ball Express building.

Nazi Headquarters

After many failed attempts to take over Marwencol, the Nazis were weary of holding their meetings in their Kübelwagens, so they constructed their own rudimentary headquarters on the outskirts of town. In front of the headquarters, there is a large boulder to which the Nazis chain their prisoners. If the prisoner can pull the rock, he is free to go.

Guard Shack and Gate

The Marwencol guard shack and gate features a working gate arm and lights. It sits across from Marwencol's only stoplight, which is also wired with real lights. Mark built the guard shack out of found wood and old roof tiles that he trimmed to fit. The black stripes on the gate arm were created with electrical tape.

Nazi Encampment

The Nazis set up a comfortable encampment outside of town (in Mark's front yard) in addition to their headquarters. The tents, which were gifts from Marwencol fans, were built on wood and brick foundations to prevent plants from growing inside, and were erected months ahead of Mark's photo shoot so they would be properly weathered and camouflaged by plants. He covered them with netting that was formerly a decorative fishing net from the Anchorage. Inside one of the tents is a working wood stove outfitted with a tea light for warmth.

Adolf Hitler and his men at work in the Nazi headquarters formulating a plan to capture Marwencol.

A Nazi bike messenger blows through Marwencol's guard gate.

G6
7.1

CHAPTER EIGHT

Characters

"When I get a new character and open up that box, the first thing I look at is its face. Whoever the figure looks like, that becomes its alter ego. // Sometimes I look online for a character that resembles a friend of mine because I want that person in Marwencol. And sometimes my friends—like the guys in the club—will send me a figure that looks like them so I can put them in my town. // When I pick up that figure and it's an alter ego of one of my friends, I know their personalities, so I just transform it into the doll in my mind. So the doll does things that the person would do in real life…and sometimes a little bit more. And in my mind, they have real feelings. They feel anger and love; they feel jealousy and pain; and, sometimes, they want revenge."

opposite: Mark and his alter ego, Hogie, with their cameras.

Hogie sets up a scene in his miniature World War II town.

Captain "Hogie" Hogancamp

Nationality: American

Ranks: US Army Captain, US Tank Commander (as the story changes, so does Hogie's rank)

Counterpart: Mark Hogancamp

Backstory: In April 1943, Captain "Hogie" Hogancamp was flying a routine mission over China when his P-40 Warhawk was shot down, inexplicably landing in a field in Belgium. After escaping his aircraft, Hogie stumbled upon the small Belgian village of Marwencol. The female residents of the town gave him a bar, which he named Hogancamp's Ruined Stocking Catfight Club. Hogie is the perpetual target of five relentless SS soldiers. He is also beloved by two women—Anna Romanov and Deja, the Belgian Witch of Marwencol. Though he has been magically connected to Deja for more than two thousand years, his heart belongs to Anna.

(Princess) Anna Romanov

Nationality: Russian

Rank: Traffic Sergeant, Red Army

Counterpart: None

Backstory: Anna Romanov is actually Princess Anna, the daughter of Russia's king and queen, who sent her away in anticipation of a coup. After fleeing her mother Russia, Anna enlisted in the Russian army, where she was made a traffic sergeant. When war broke out, she was sent to Europe and later found her way to Marwencol, Belgium. Anna fell in love with Captain Hogancamp at first sight and won his heart by rescuing him from the SS. Hogie and Anna got married, but their relationship is constantly tested by Deja Thoris, the Belgian Witch of Marwencol.

Anna and Hogie inside the Ruined Stocking Catfight Club.

Deja Thoris arrives in her time-displacement machine to save Hogie.

Dej'Alaqua Montique "Deja" Thoris

Nationality: Belgian

Title: The Belgian Witch of Marwencol

Counterpart: None

Backstory: Dej'Alaqua Montique "Deja" Thoris was born thousands of years ago in another dimension to a sorcerer father and witch mother. She has two sisters—Agatha (also a witch) and Dahlia. Deja first met Hogie around 2,700 years ago. Believing him to be her soul mate, she chased him through time, ultimately landing in Marwencol. Deja uses a time-displacement machine and casts spells with the help of magical gloves. Her gloves give her innumerable powers, including the power to banish people from Marwencol to the land of the Knight of Marwencol. Unfortunately, her powers don't work in the real 1:1 scale world, where Deja relies on the protection of the Giant of Marwencol—who is Mark himself.

Mark's German maternal grandparents, "Omi" and "Papi," during World War II.

Grandpa "Papi" Ewald

"When I'm working on the town, and I can't get a German figure set up right or I'm missing a piece of something he should be carrying, my German grandfather's voice comes into my head and tells me, 'No, you gotta put this on and take this off. We didn't wear those things.' // My German grandfather, 'Papi,' was in the Luftwaffe during World War II. He told me he, as a young teen, was working to get his degree in mechanics, so he went to mechanic school, and when he finished, he got his diploma. It was mandatory at that time in Germany for every youngster or teenager when you were of age to do two years in the military. So my grandfather did that, and while he was in the Luftwaffe, the war broke out. So he was sucked into the war—he didn't join. He was a mechanic for the antiaircraft guns, and he rode around on a BMW motorcycle with a sidecar. // I asked him one time, 'Did you ever have a machine gun on the sidecar? And he said, 'No, no, I carried all my tools in the sidecar to repair the guns. I didn't put a machine gun on the sidecar until we went through Belgium.' Maybe that's one reason I set Marwencol in Belgium."

"My grandfathers repairing the Spitfire for the injured Scott Merry."

"Wendy, Colleen, and I look out over my bar."

Wendy

Nationality: American

Title: Civilian owner of Wendy Lee's Kitchen

Counterpart: Wendy, former waitress and hostess at the Anchorage Restaurant

Backstory: Wendy was one of the many female residents of Marwencol who hid during the SS siege of Marwencol. She owned and operated the former Wendy Lee's Kitchen. Together with Colleen and Mark, Wendy's name forms a part of the town's name, Marwencol.

Colleen

Nationality: American

Title: Civilian owner of Pocket Full of Posies

Counterpart: Mark's former neighbor

Backstory: Colleen was the owner of Marwencol's former gift shop, Pocket Full of Posies. Shortly after Captain Hogancamp discovered Marwencol, he and Colleen dated and were engaged. When their brief engagement ended, Colleen was sent to a parallel universe by Deja Thoris, the Belgian Witch of Marwencol, and Pocket Full of Posies was transformed into a brothel.

L5
WAR-TOYS
USPS
GERMAN FALLSCHIRMJAEGER
TO: HOGIE 309
MARWENCOL
BELGIUM

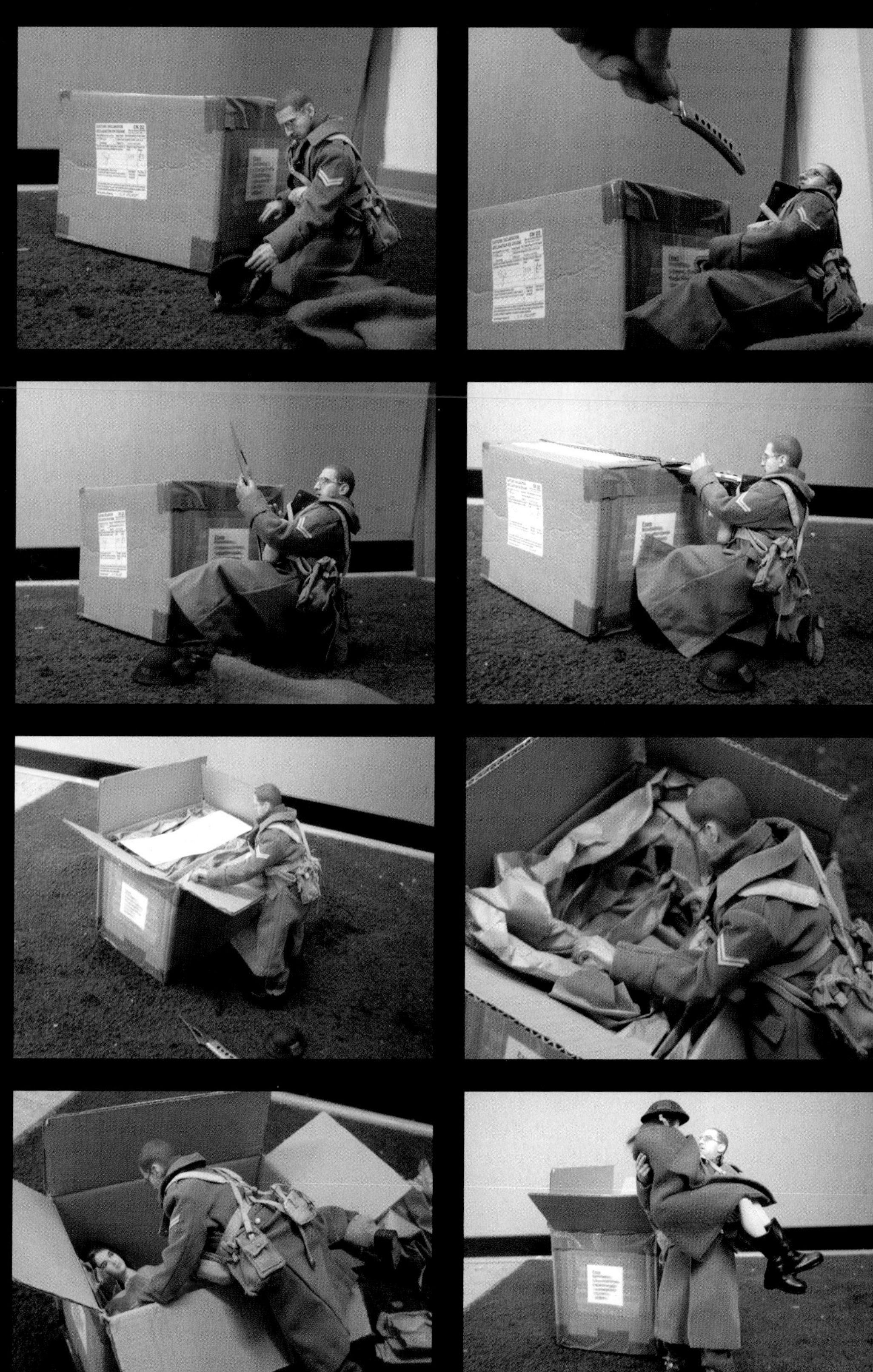

Mom is a German civilian based on Mark's mother, Edda. She assists as a bartender, a nurse, and a Nazi killer—"Verever there is trouble."

Gregg is an American military police officer based on Mark's brother Gregg. He is one of Hogie's two bodyguards, fending off the SS soldiers who hunt his brother.

Mike is an American military police officer based on Mark's brother Mike. He works alongside Gregg on Hogie's bodyguard team.

Grandpa Hogancamp is a Polish mechanic based on Mark's Polish grandfather. He works at Hogancamp's Red Ball Express with Papi.

The Professor is based on a friend of Mark's from the Ultimate Soldier website. Originally a German sniper, he became the postmaster general of Marwencol, known as Mailman, after the death of Ruthie.

Hayden, the Ghost of Marwencol, is the lone reminder of those who died at the hands of the Nazis in Marwencol. She is visible only to Deja Thoris and the Giant of Marwencol.

Tod is an American medic based on Tod Lippy, editor of *Esopus* magazine. Tod is a Red Cross medical officer in Marwencol.

Jeff is an Associated Press director based on Jeff Malmberg, the director of *Marwencol*. A former German propaganda director, Jeff switched sides to work for the AP.

Ruthie is a Belgian civilian based on Mark's friend and former coworker Ruthie. She is the paramour of a German sniper named the Professor.

Tonjes is an American civilian based on a friend of Mark's from the Ultimate Soldier website. He is a carpenter and sculptor who owns Tonjes's Furniture in Marwencol.

Chris is based on Chris Shellen, the coauthor of this book. She lives and works with her husband Jeff in Malmberg Film Studios, where she regularly throws parties for the residents of Marwencol.

Ten Bears is the daughter of Chief Great Bear, created to honor Mark's paternal Native American roots. A powerful warrior, Ten Bears is named after the brave Comanche chief Ten Bears, who was also a character in *The Outlaw Josey Wales*.

The German Schutzstaffel (the SS)

Nationality: German

Counterparts: Mark's attackers

Backstory: The German Schutzstaffel (the SS) began as Hitler's personal guard and became known as the deadliest and more zealous of Germany's World War II military forces. Before Captain Hogancamp's crash landing, the SS swept through Marwencol, executing men, women, and children. Hogie and the women of Marwencol rebuilt the town, but the SS soon returned. Unlike the Wehrmacht (regular German soldiers), the SS are not placated by booze and catfights; they want blood, specifically that of Captain Hogancamp, whom they hunt relentlessly. The SS in Marwencol possess special powers that enable them to come back to life—"respawn"—when killed.
To eliminate an SS soldier from Marwencol forever, they must be banished to another dimension by Deja Thoris, and beheaded by the mythical Knight of Marwencol.

The Knight of Marwencol

Nationality: Unknown

Rank: Knight

Counterpart: None

Backstory: The Knight of Marwencol lives in a parallel universe—a mythical land of green hills and blue skies. His identity is a secret to everyone except Deja Thoris. When someone misbehaves in Marwencol, Deja has the power to magically transport them to the land of the Knight of Marwencol, where justice is swiftly dealt by the knight's sword. Once someone is beheaded by the knight, they can never return to Marwencol. It is the only way to permanently kill a member of the SS.

A.

B.

A. Hitler and his men walking into Marwencol.

B. A curious SS soldier interrupts the women of Marwencol as they bathe together in the river.

C.

D.

Green Leader (G. L.)

Nationality: American

Rank: Three-Star General

Counterpart: Green Leader, head of the Ultimate Soldier website

Backstory: Green Leader (G. L.) is Marwencol's highest-ranking American soldier, leading Hogie and his fellow troops in battle.

The Ultimate Soldiers

Mark met some of Marwencol's most important residents through the Ultimate Soldier website. Led by G. L., these men come from around the world to serve in key positions throughout Marwencol.

Some of the Ultimate Soldiers include, from left to right, ILAF, Rich, Mailman, Medi-Jeep, Irish, Tank Mechanic, Greaylin, Tonjes, Sgt. Howard, Warriors 1st BN, B. C. Ries, Storm, and Mike.

A.

B.

C.

D.

"Pvt. Mel and Sgt. Howard are warned to get out of Belgium by Mel's mom."

"T. C. and I are sitting drinking real coffee under our shelter made of bodies during the worst snowstorm in Belgian history. The real T. C. died before this was taken, but he lives on in Marwencol."

"Irish wishes me good luck before I take off on my next mission."

Part III

MARWENCOL STORIES

"MARWENCOL"

BELGIUM

BY

MARK EDWARD HOGANCAMP

2003-

"To anyone, with an imagination."

Mark E. Hogancamp

"It was April 1943 and the people of Marwencol were just sitting down for their evening meal when the Germans rolled into town. Life stopped for a moment, as if someone had pressed a pause button. // The townspeople had only heard about the war; they never thought they would actually see someone from it. They knew that the soldiers were German. What they didn't know was that they were the meanest, most uncaring, and rotten men that ever came out of the SS. And they were lost and angry. // The Germans grew more annoyed with the townspeople by the minute. Every time the soldiers demanded that someone show them where they were—where Marwencol was—on the map, the people said, 'I don't know.' // So the soldiers ate whatever they wanted, took whatever they wanted, and did whatever they felt like doing in the town. When they finished, they started killing the elders of the town. Then they killed the men. And then they raped and killed the young women. // When the SS were finished eliminating everyone, they left. They left the town empty and desolate. This town, Marwencol, was a ghost town. Barren and devoid of life. And that's when Hogie came into the picture."

CRASH LANDING

I CAME FLYING OVER IN MY P-40 WARHAWK, ON FIRE. I SAW A FLAT FIELD AND A TOWN BELOW. I DIDN'T EVEN KNOW THERE WAS A TOWN IN THIS AREA. ALL I KNEW WAS I HAD TO PUT HER DOWN SOMEWHERE. SO I CRASH-LANDED.

183
POISON

HUGIE'S
183

HUGIE'S
NO PUSH

AT FIRST THERE WAS NOBODY AROUND...

THEN, ONE BY ONE, BEAUTIFUL, DOLL-LIKE WOMEN STARTED TO EMERGE...

WE DROVE INTO TOWN, BUT THERE WASN'T ANYONE AROUND...

THE SS, I FOUND OUT LATER, HAD GONE THROUGH MARWENCOL AND KILLED THE MEN, WOMEN, AND CHILDREN.

IT WAS A DESOLATE TOWN.

SLOWLY...WOMEN STARTED TO COME OUT. THEY'D HIDDEN WHEN THE SS CAME THROUGH.

THEY ALL CAME OUT AND THANKED ME...JUST ME AND TWENTY-SEVEN WOMEN...I WAS THINKING, BOY, WHAT A LUCKY GUY I AM.

HOGANCAMP'S
309
THEY GAVE ME MY OWN PLACE, MY OWN BUILDING, WHICH I TURNED INTO A BAR.

THE RULES
OF TOWN

MEANWHILE, SOLDIERS STARTED
WANDERING INTO MARWENCOL...

T
zur Rollbahn
Petersburg-Moskau

PEOPLE KEPT TRICKLING IN...GERMANS, AMERICANS...OTHER LOST PATROLS.

MARWENCO

I TOLD THEM THERE WAS ONLY ONE RULE IN MY TOWN: BE FRIENDLY WITH EACH OTHER.

SO THEY WERE.

THE AMERICANS.

THE BRITISH.

THE GERMANS.

THEY ALL DRANK TOGETHER, SMOKED TOGETHER.

Heineken
IT DIDN'T MATTER WHAT KIND OF CLOTHING THEY WORE.

NOBODY WAS AGAINST ANYBODY.

EVEN THE TOWN GERMANS...
Heineken

I TOLD THEM TO BEHAVE.

BELGIUM
HOGAN CAMP
309
AND AS LONG AS I GAVE THEM BOOZE AND A COUPLE OF STAGED CATFIGHTS, EVERYBODY WAS HAPPY.

EVERYBODY GOT ALONG...
EVERYBODY BUT THE SS.

THE SS EVENTUALLY HEARD ABOUT MY TOWN...MY BAR.
THEY HEARD ABOUT THE WOMEN—THAT THE MARWENCOL
WOMEN WERE THE MOST BEAUTIFUL IN BELGIUM.

THE SS FIND
MARWENCOL

THEY WERE DRIVING AROUND AIMLESSLY...

Malmedy
Elsenborn
250 km.

Elsenborn
250 km.

...BUT EVENTUALLY THEY FOUND MY TOWN.

THERE WAS NO ONE AROUND. WE WERE HIDING IN THE BAR, TWO MILES AWAY.

RUTHIE...
SHE'D STAYED BEHIND TO 
WATCH OVER THE CHURCH.

THEY INTERROGATED HER, BUT
STILL SHE WOULDN'T TALK.

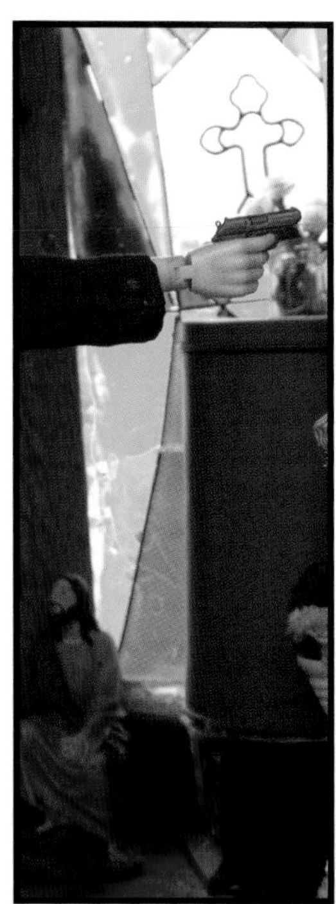

SO THEY SHOT HER.

OUTSIDE, THE PROFESSOR HAD
COME BACK TO CHECK ON RUTHIE.

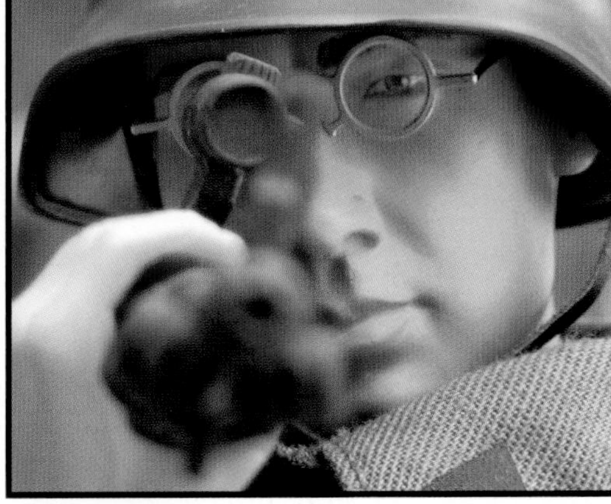

BY ONE.

HE GOT THREE OF THEM UNTIL THE SS SCURRIED BACK INTO THE CHURCH.

ONE OF THE SS SAW HIM AND TOOK A SHOT.

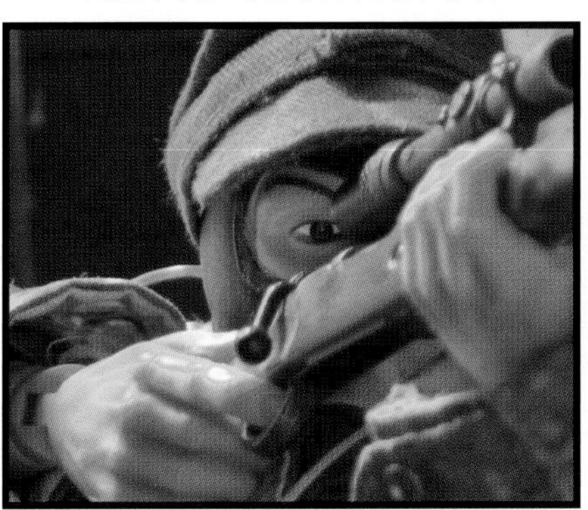

THE PROFESSOR
WAS DOWN.

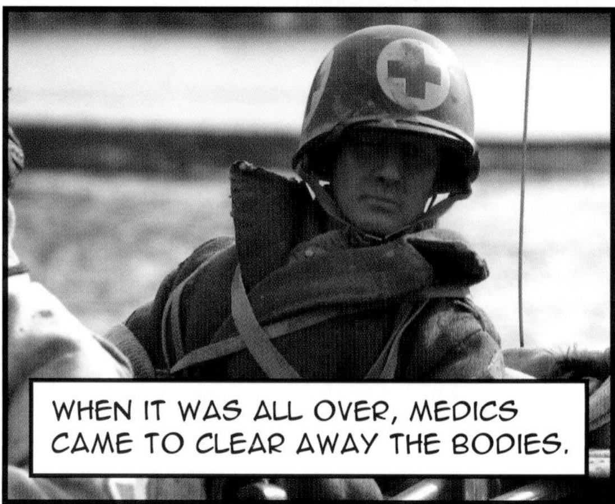
WHEN IT WAS ALL OVER, MEDICS
CAME TO CLEAR AWAY THE BODIES.

'POCKET
FULL OF
POSIES'

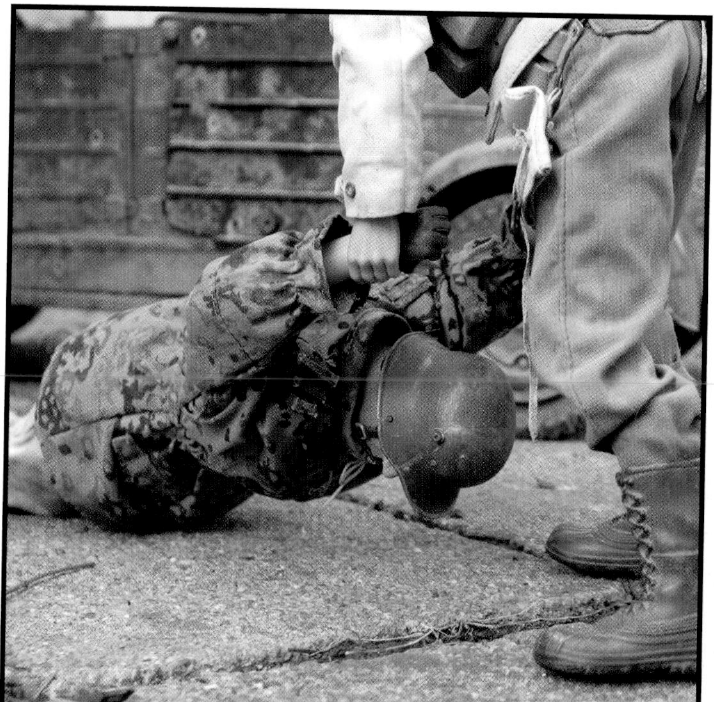

THEN ONE OF THE CREW MEMBERS SPOTTED A SURVIVOR...

...THE PROFESSOR WAS ALIVE!

THE
PRISONER

BACK AT MY BAR, WE HEARD ABOUT
RUTHIE AND THE PROFESSOR.

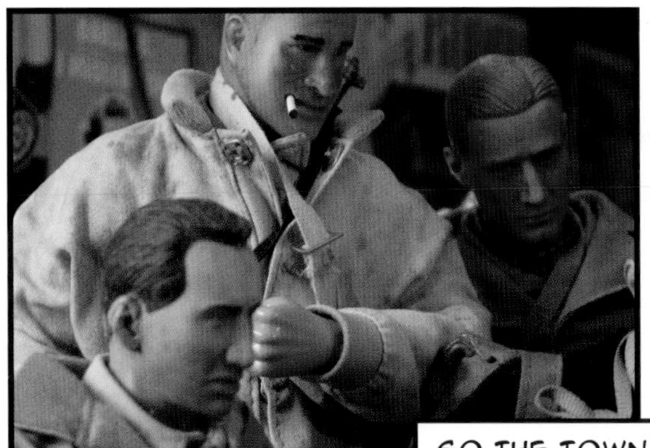

SO THE TOWN GERMANS
AND I CAME UP WITH A PLAN.

PETROL STATION
BANK

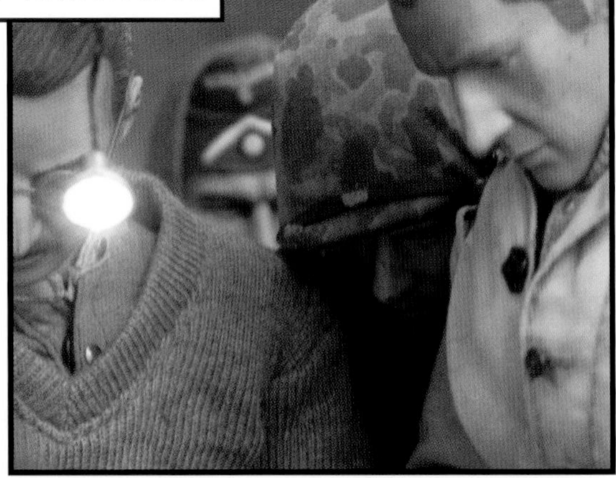

OPERATION: BROKEN ARROW

I WOULD PRETEND TO BE THEIR PRISONER, AND THEY WOULD BRING ME TO THE CHURCH. THAT WAY, WE COULD INFILTRATE THE SS AND GET OUR TOWN BACK.

THE SS TOOK ME AND SENT THE TOWN GERMANS AWAY.

THEY TIED ME UP AND STARTED INTERROGATING ME...CUTTING ME...

WHERE'S THE BAR?!

MEANWHILE, WORD GOT BACK TO THE DOLLS AT MY BAR THAT THE SS HAD ME TIED UP AND WERE CUTTING ME TO RIBBONS. MY GIRLFRIEND, ANNA, DIDN'T WANT TO WAIT FOR ANOTHER BRILLIANT PLAN FROM THE TOWNSPEOPLE. SO SHE TOOK CHRIS AND JACQUELINE AND TRADED THEIR UNIFORMS FOR DOLL CLOTHES.

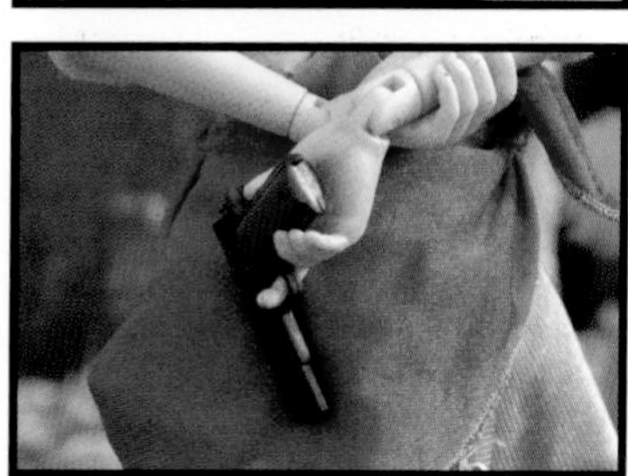

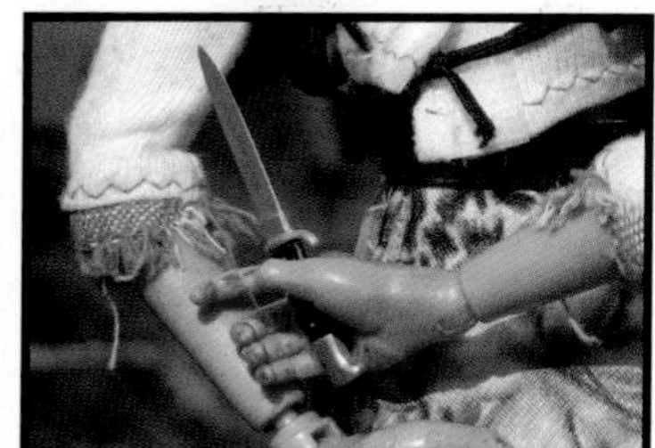

...ANNA RECOVERED MY REVOLVER.

THEY WENT INTO THE CHURCH, AND JUST LIKE PRECISION SURGEONS...

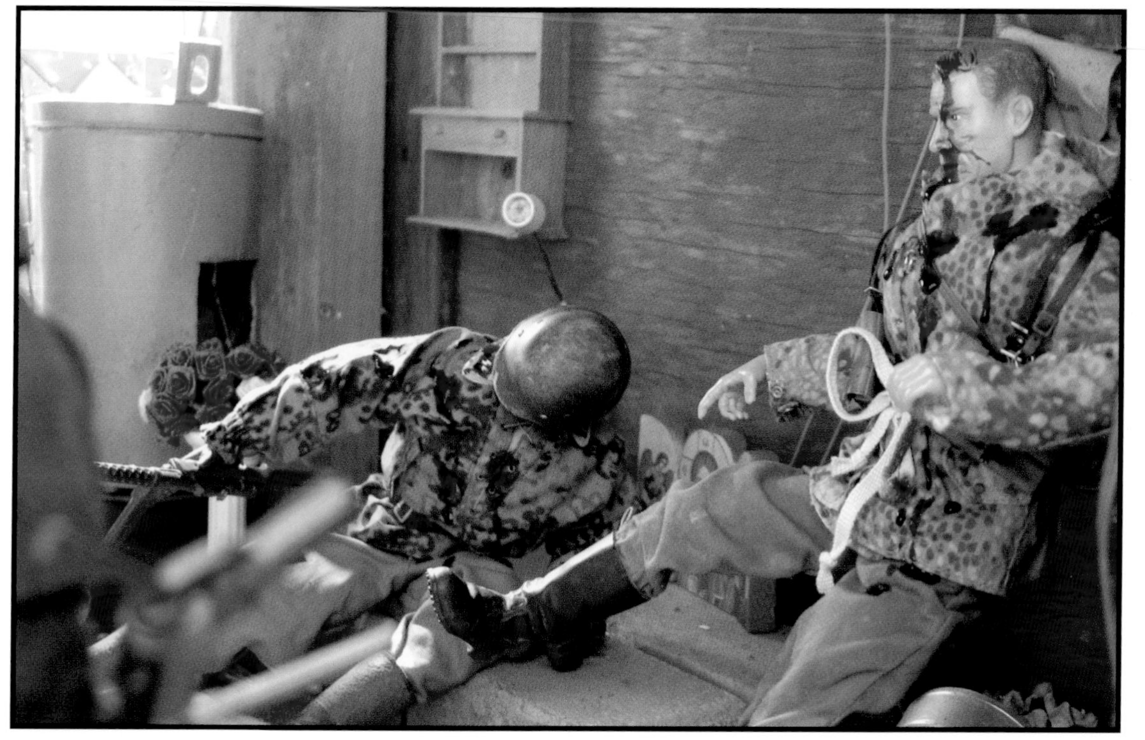

THEY ONLY WOUNDED
THE WORST SS GUY.

THEY HAD PLANS FOR HIM.

THEY WERE GOING TO
SAVE HIM FOR LATER.

AND THEN ANNA CAME
OVER AND CUT ME DOWN.

SHE HELD ME UNTIL THE
JEEP CAME TO TAKE
US BACK TO THE BAR.

HER SAVING ME
PROVED TO ME THAT
SHE LOVED ME...
IT PROVED THAT SHE
FELT THE SAME WAY
I FELT ABOUT HER.

LATER, THE CALL WENT OUT TO THE WOMEN OF MARWENCOL.

IT WAS LIKE SOMETHING OUT OF *MACBETH*.

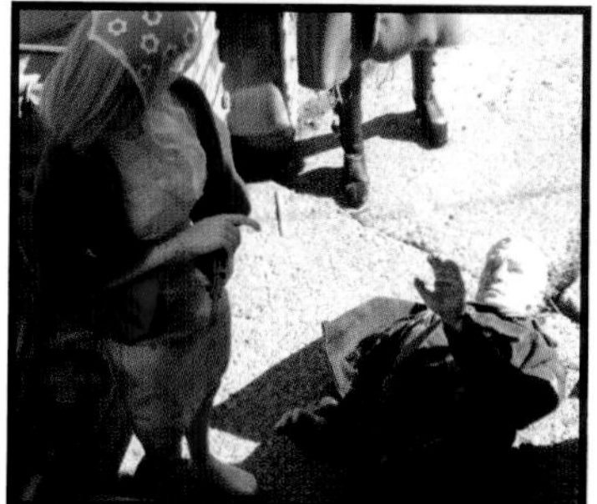

THEN SVETLANA TOOK A PISTOL WHILE THE GUY WAS STILL ALIVE.

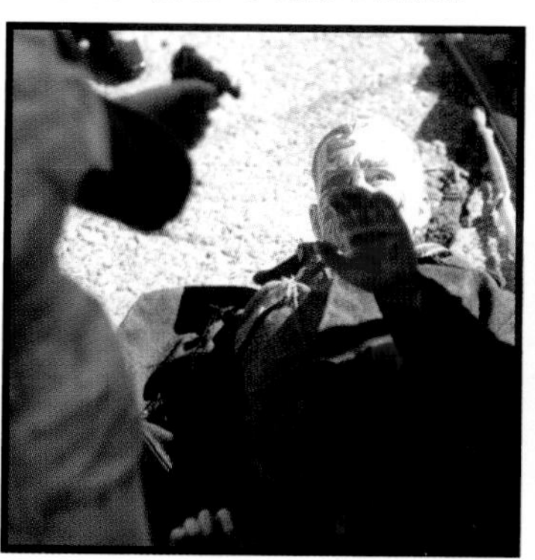

THE SS THAT ATTACKED MARWENCOL WERE HUNG UPSIDE
DOWN IN TOWN. THIS WAS TO SHOW THE OTHER NAZIS THE
TREATMENT THEY WOULD RECEIVE IF THEY MESSED WITH US.

ANNA SAW IT AND REALIZED...

BENJERMIN COLE
PVT. U.S. ARMY
...IT WAS THE PERFECT BACKDROP FOR OUR WEDDING.

DEJA JUMPED INTO HER TIME-DISPLACEMENT MACHINE, WHICH ALLOWS HER TO MANIPULATE TIME FOR HER OWN PURPOSES...

...LIKE SENDING ME BACK IN TIME SO I WOULDN'T MEET ANNA!

CLANG CLANG
USA 3047999
A NEW BEGINNING

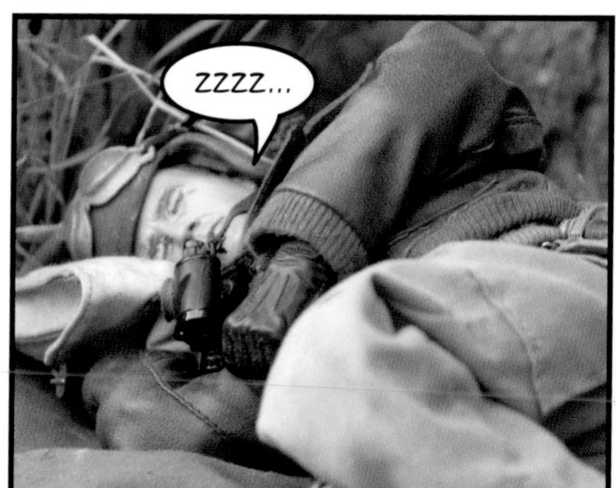
ZZZZ...

A-HA!

CLINK CLANK

TANK'S FIXED!
USA 3047

'EY HOGIE, WAKE UP!

C'MON BUDDY,
WE GOTTA GO.

HOW LONG
HAVE I BEEN
ASLEEP?

'BOUT SIX
HOURS. WHY?

I JUST DREAMT SIX YEARS OF LIFE... IN SIX HOURS?

WHAT D'YA MEAN?
USA 30479

I WAS A FLYING TIGERS PILOT, AND I FOUND A TOWN FULL OF BEAUTIFUL WOMEN...

THAT'S SOME DREAM! C'MON, LET'S GO FIND THE WAR.

USA 3047999

15
I COULDN'T BELIEVE IT HAD ALL BEEN A DREAM. I CLIMBED INTO THE TANK, AND SGT. HOWARD, TANK MECHANIC, AND I SET OUT TO FIND SOME ACTION.

ALONG THE WAY, WE CAME ACROSS
A BEAUTIFUL WOMAN WITH BLUE HAIR.

BELGIUM
Zeebrugge
Blankenberge
Ostend
Knokke
Bruges
Diksmuide
Ypres
Mouscron
Kortrijk
Tournai
Ghent
Brussels
FRANCE

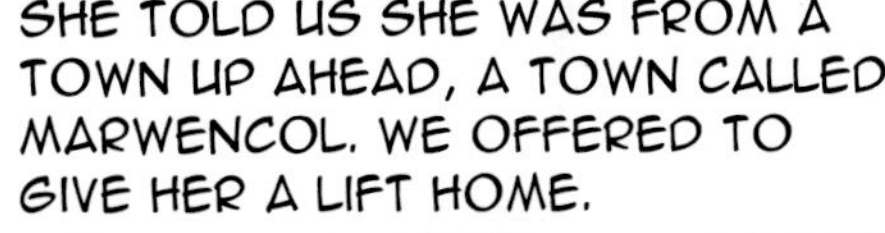
SHE TOLD US SHE WAS FROM A
TOWN UP AHEAD, A TOWN CALLED
MARWENCOL. WE OFFERED TO
GIVE HER A LIFT HOME.

SHE LOOKED SO FAMILIAR...

HE WAS GOING TO COME IN REAL HANDY WHEN WE GOT TO MARWENCOL.

YOU SEE, THE TOWN HAD BEEN OCCUPIED BY NAZIS, WHO WERE HOLDING THE TOWNSPEOPLE HOSTAGE INSIDE MARWENCOL...

THEY CONTROLLED THE ENTIRE TOWN. THEY'D EVEN STATIONED A GUARD IN THE FRONT GUARD GATE.

BUT WE WERE READY FOR THEM.

...AND BLEW THE GUARD AWAY.

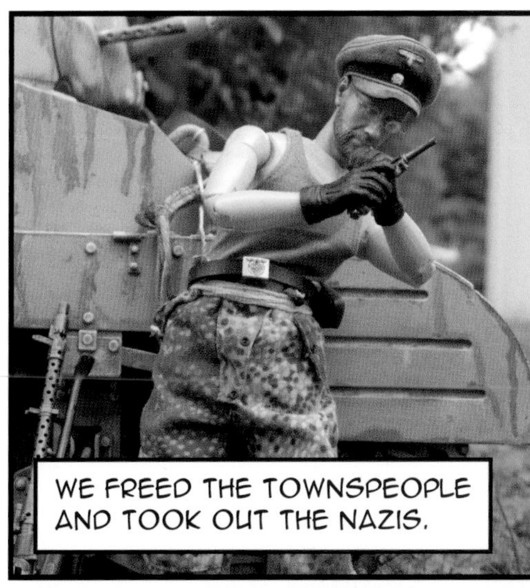
WE FREED THE TOWNSPEOPLE
AND TOOK OUT THE NAZIS.

THEY DIDN'T STAND
A CHANCE.

Military ★ Star

Victory! AT MARWENCOL

THE NAZIS WERE FURIOUS, BUT THEY HAD ONE MORE TRICK UP THEIR SLEEVE...

...DEEP IN THE FOREST, THEY
WERE HOLDING A HOSTAGE.

WE ORGANIZED A RESCUE TEAM AND CAME UP FROM THE RIVER.
TEN BEARS CAME UP FROM THE OTHER SIDE.
SCHHWAFFT

THEN THE BATTLE BEGAN...

AFTER IT WAS OVER, CHRIS CAME OVER AND UNMASKED THE HOSTAGE.
HER NAME WAS ANNA.

WHEN THE CROWD PARTED, WE SAW EACH OTHER FOR THE FIRST TIME...
...IT WAS LOVE AT FIRST SIGHT.

WHEN WE KISSED, ANNA AND I REMEMBERED ALL THE LOVE WE ONCE FELT AND DEJA'S SPELL WAS BROKEN. IT SEEMED LIKE EVERYTHING WOULD FINALLY GO BACK TO NORMAL.

BUT LIFE IN MARWENCOL WAS ABOUT TO GET EVEN STRANGER.

DAHLIA
INTERNATIONAL CRIMINAL DAHLIA THORIS HAD JUST ROBBED A BANK IN MODERN-DAY GERMANY. SHE SPED OFF ON HER MOTORCYCLE WITH THE GERMAN POLICE IN HOT PURSUIT.

SHE CAME SCREECHING AROUND A CORNER AND SPOTTED A TOWN AHEAD, BUT SHE DIDN'T SEE THE GROUP OF SS SOLDIERS ON THE ROAD.

SHE CRASHED HEADFIRST INTO DEMETRIE AND FLEW OVER THE HANDLEBARS OF HER MOTORCYCLE WITH HER BAG OF CASH.

THE GERMAN COPS ARRIVED AND SAW THE SS BUT FIGURED IT WAS A WAR REENACTMENT. THEY JUMPED OUT AND DREW THEIR GUNS ON DAHLIA.

DAHLIA GOT UP ONTO HER HANDS AND KNEES...

AND CAME UP FIRING...

BLAM!
BLAM!
BLAM!

THE NAZIS DIDN'T KNOW THE COPS WERE GERMAN, SO THEY JOINED IN.

BLAM!

BUT THEN DAHLIA SHOT THEM TOO.
ONCE EVERYONE WAS DEAD, DAHLIA PUT HER GUN AWAY...

SHE RIGHTED
HER BIKE...

...AND SHOT
OUT OF TOWN.

BUT JUST AS DAHLIA
ROUNDED THE CORNER...
CRASH!!
UNIT PRO-LINK
PHANOM

SHE HIT THE INSIDE OF
THE MARWENCOL DOME.

SHE REACHED UP AND FELT THE SURFACE OF THE DOME.

SHE COULD SEE THE OUTSIDE WORLD SHE'D JUST COME FROM, BUT SHE COULDN'T GET OUT THERE.

THEN DAHLIA LOOKED AROUND AND SAW A LADY WITH BLUE HAIR.

DEJA?

HELLO, DEAR SISTER.

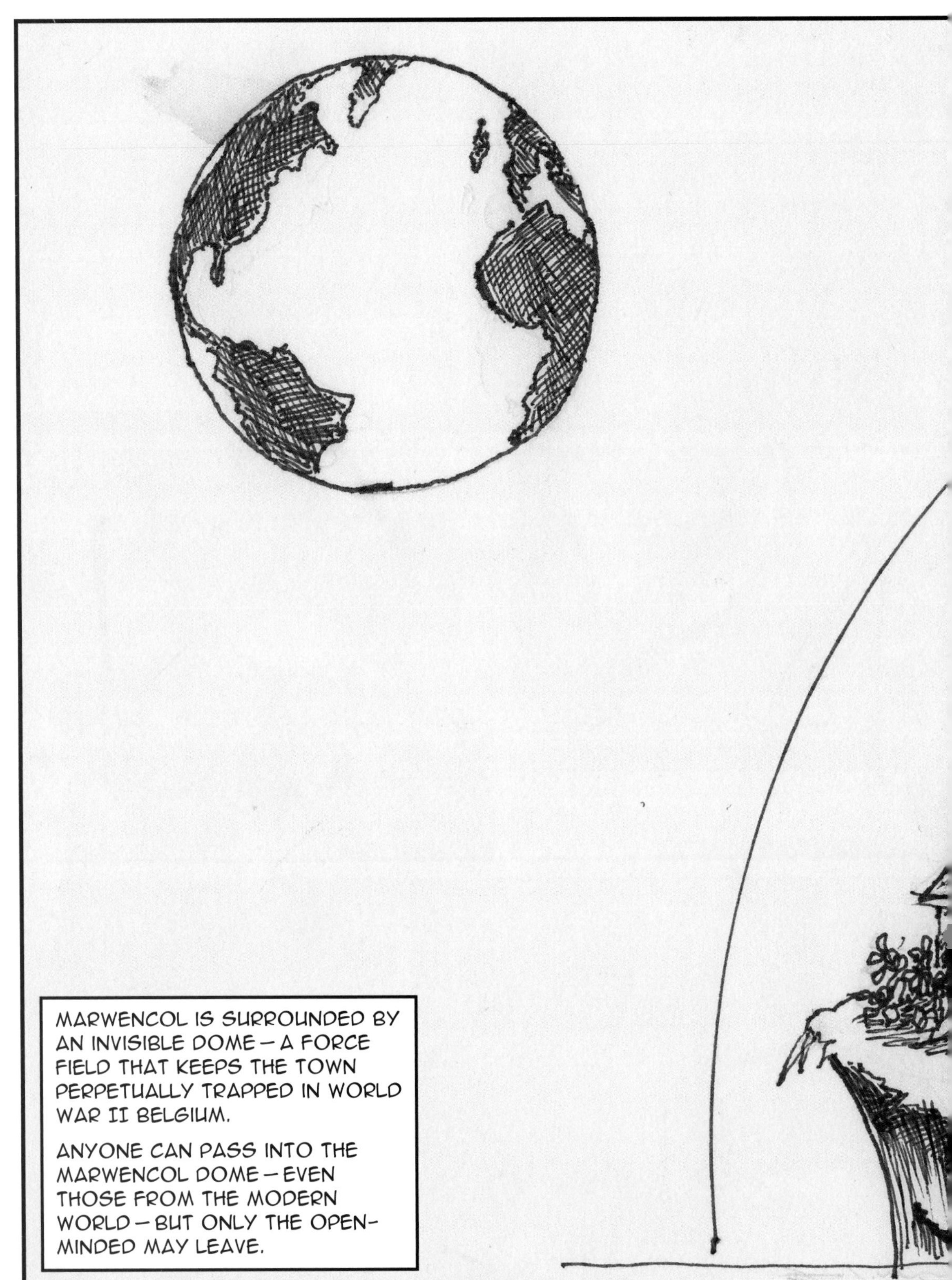
MARWENCOL IS SURROUNDED BY AN INVISIBLE DOME—A FORCE FIELD THAT KEEPS THE TOWN PERPETUALLY TRAPPED IN WORLD WAR II BELGIUM.
ANYONE CAN PASS INTO THE MARWENCOL DOME—EVEN THOSE FROM THE MODERN WORLD—BUT ONLY THE OPEN-MINDED MAY LEAVE.

Mark E. Hogancamp
2013

THE SISTERS WALKED UP MAIN STREET TO FIX DAHLIA'S BIKE.
SHE DIED LAST YEAR. SHE ASKED FOR YOU.
WHAT'S UP WITH THIS PLACE? AND HOW'S MOM?
SUDDENLY, SOMETHING AHEAD MADE DAHLIA STOP IN HER TRACKS.

SINCE THE MODERN GERMAN COPS WERE FROM THE OUTSIDE WORLD, THEY WERE DEAD. BUT THE WORLD WAR II NAZIS FROM MARWENCOL RESPAWN AFTER THEIR DEATHS.

THEY JUST GOT UP, DUSTED THEMSELVES OFF, AND WALKED AWAY.

ANOTHER NAZI HAD BEEN BURIED FOR TWO YEARS. JEEPS AND TRUCKS HAD FLATTENED HIM INTO THE GROUND. BUT EVIL NEVER DIES IN MARWENCOL...

SUDDENLY, THE SOLDIER SPOTTED THE TOWN FOUNTAIN.

AFTER BEING BURIED FOR TWO YEARS, HE WANTED SOME WATER. BUT DAHLIA HAD OTHER PLANS...

BLAM!
BLAM!

THAT, DEAR SISTER, IS HOW I GET THINGS DONE.

WHAT THE HELL?!!

ONLY ONE THING CAN KILL THE NAZIS IN MARWENCOL...AND IT ISN'T BULLETS.

THIS, DEAR DAHLIA, IS HOW WE DO THINGS IN MARWENCOL.

POOFFF

???
IN A FLASH, DEJA ZAPPED THE SS SOLDIER INTO THE LAND OF THE KNIGHT OF MARWENCOL.

THE KNIGHT RODE UP
SILENTLY BEHIND HIM...

FSSHT!!

NOW DECAPITATED, THE SS SOLDIER COULD NEVER RETURN TO THE STORY AGAIN...

THE MYSTERIOUS KNIGHT HAD STRUCK AGAIN...

THE SS WERE STILL AFTER ME, SO THEY KIDNAPPED DEJA AND HER FRIEND AVA.

THE GIANT OF
MARWENCOL

TELL US WHERE
HE IS, WITCH!

DEJA STAYED SILENT, SO
THE SS HUMILIATED THEM...

...BUT STILL DEJA WOULDN'T TALK.

SO THE SS TORTURED THEM.

WHP-EESH!

BUT INSTEAD OF TELLING THEM WHERE I WAS, DEJA STARTED TO CHANT, "OH, MY LOVE, HEAR ME...SHOW NO MERCY. DO NOT FORGIVE THEM, MY LOVE. I BEG OF YOU...LAY THY HAND UPON THESE MEN WITH A GIANT VENGEANCE AND WRATH!"

A GIANT HAND APPEARED
AND, WITH A TOUCH...

...HE TOOK THEIR SOULS FROM THEIR
BODIES AND SENT THEM TO HELL.

THE BODIES OF THE NAZIS
DROPPED WHERE THEY STOOD...

...INTO THE MUD, WHERE
THEY BELONGED.

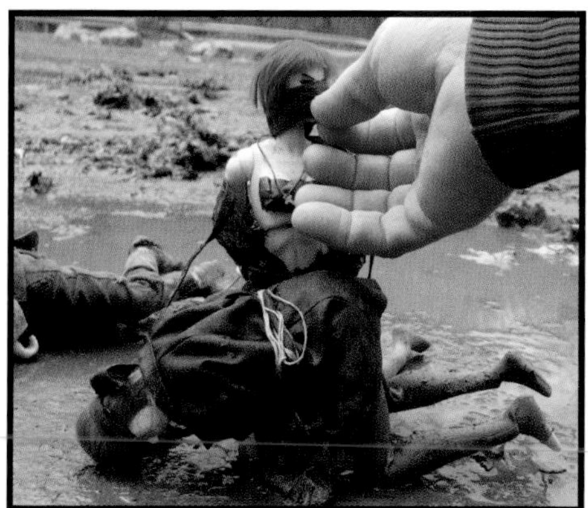

THEN HE CAREFULLY TOOK OFF THE GIRLS' GAGS AND BLINDFOLDS.

DEJA
HOGANCAMP
AFTER THE GIANT SAVED DEJA FROM THE SS, SHE PROPOSED TO HIM. THEY WERE MARRIED ON HIS BIRTHDAY—MARCH 20—SO THEY WOULD NEVER FORGET THEIR ANNIVERSARY.

EVERYONE IN MARWENCOL WAS INVITED,
BUT ONLY FOUR PEOPLE SHOWED UP...

ME, MAXIMILIAN,
ANNA'S BODYGUARD...

...AND HAYDEN, THE
GHOST OF MARWENCOL.

WE WERE THE ONLY FOUR WHO
BELIEVED IN A HUMAN BEING
MARRYING A 1:6 SCALE DOLL.

AFTER THE VOWS, THE GIANT RAISED DEJA'S VEIL SO EVERYONE COULD SEE HER FACE.

MEANWHILE, AN SS SOLDIER SNUCK UP ON US WITH A GRENADE.

JUST AS HE WAS READY TO PULL THE CORD, THE GIANT EXCUSED HIMSELF AND WALKED AROUND TO THE FRONT OF THE CHURCH.

THE GIANT REACHED DOWN...

...GRABBED THE SS SOLDIER...

...AND SQUASHED
HIM OUT OF SIGHT.

THEN THE GIANT CAME BACK.

HE CARRIED HIS BRIDE OUT TO
THE FRONT OF THE CHURCH...

...TO START THEIR NEW LIFE
TOGETHER AS MAN AND WIFE,
IN HIS WORLD AND HERS.
TO BE
CONTINUED...

Figure Details

Captain Hogancamp
"Tom," US 82nd Airborne Pathfinder, Dragon Models Limited

Deja Thoris
"Alaqua," Dark Desires Cy Girl, Blue Box International

Anna Romanov
"Anna," Red Army NCO Traffic Control Branch, Dragon Models Limited

Hayden, the Ghost of Marwencol
"Subject 1025: The Babysitter," Sideshow Collectibles

Wendy & Colleen
Mattel Barbie dolls

Edda, Hogie's Mother
"Pussy Galore," James Bond Goldfinger, Sideshow Collectibles

Other Characters
Assorted figures from:
21st Century Toys
Blue Box International
Dragon Models Limited
Mattel
Sideshow Collectibles
Tonner Doll Company

Photo Details

All photos by Mark Hogancamp unless otherwise noted.

Page 1: "Jeff turns the camera around after taking a picture of the dead SS."

Page 10: A box of figures awaiting a scene. (Photo by Chris Shellen)

Page 71: The photo of American GIs was taken only a few months before the printing of this book.

Process
Page 80: Mark photographing a scene in Marwencol in 2009. (Photo of Mark by Jeff Malmberg)

Page 81: A photo of Anna from the scene in Marwencol, 2009.

Stories—Crash Landing
Page 148–49: Mark painted and weathered Hogie's P-40 before shooting it. The propeller is actually spinning.

Page 150: Mark didn't own any 1:6 scale planes until 2010, so the photos of Hogie's P-40 plane were taken in 2013, six years after he shot the rest of the story.

Page 152: At the bottom of the photo of Marwencol's main street, you'll see a soldier buried in the mud. That is the same SS soldier who later respawns in the story "Dahlia."

Stories—Rules of Town
Page 163: The exterior bar photo of the Ruined Stocking was taken after Mark moved his bar inside. You can see the wall of his trailer in the background.

Stories—The SS Find Marwencol
Page 166: The River Mulva in the opening shot is actually a creek near Mark's home.

Stories—The Prisoner
Page 178: Mark redraws new maps of Marwencol whenever a story calls for one.

Page 182: The scar down Hogie's face is in the same place where Mark had surgery to repair his eye after the attack.

Page 195: The tear on Deja's face is a drop of water.

Page 195: Deja's time-displacement machine was made out of an old VCR that ate one of Mark's videotapes.

opposite: Marwencol figures in Mark's home being prepped for a scene. (photo by Chris Shellen)

Stories—A New Beginning

Page 197: Sgt. Howard and Tank Mechanic are members of the Ultimate Soldier fan forum.

Page 198: Before Sgt. Howard wakes Hogie up, Hogie's eyes are "shut" with Sculpey clay.

Page 200: Mark weathered the tank using steel wool and rust-colored paint. Near the top left, you can see the faint remnant of the tank's former name, *Colleen*.

Page 212–13: Mark composed this shot to juxtapose the chaos of battle against the tranquility of nature.

Stories—Dahlia Thoris

Page 218: Dahlia is the "black sheep witch of the Thoris family."

Page 225: The Marwencol dome is actually a discarded windowpane.

Page 235: Decapitated figures are buried in Marwencol Cemetery.

Page 256: The final page of a war story from Mark's diary from the 1980s.

The Modeler's Manual
Schleicher
USCO
NORMAN ROCKWELL
Finch
ESOPUS

About the Authors

Mark Hogancamp created the 1:6 scale world of Marwencol as a means of recovery from a near-fatal attack that left him with traumatic brain injury. He is currently continuing his therapy at his home outside of Kingston, New York.

Chris Shellen is a writer and filmmaker based in California. A former film development executive, she produced the award-winning 2010 documentary *Marwencol*. She and her husband/partner, Jeff Malmberg, are currently working on a new documentary set in Italy. The pair also enjoys an exciting parallel life in the world of Marwencol.

Acknowledgments

The authors would like to extend a special thanks to Jeff Malmberg, without whom this book would not exist. We would also like to thank Tod Lippy, Janet Hicks, and Eddie Mullins for their ongoing support of Marwencol; Edda Eller, David Naugle, Bert Bodie, Tom Neubauer, Julie Swarthout, and Janet and Mark Wikane for their insight into Marwencol; Emmanuel Nneji, Joan Lamb, the Ulster County District Attorney's office, Teri Shellen, Kaz Brecher, Mike Mignola, Claire Tisne Haft, Anatasha Blakely, Kirsten Wolf, and Jaime D'Alessandro for their assistance and advice; Pat Shellen for her time; our families and publisher for their continued belief in this project; and the many Marwencol Facebook fans who contributed ideas for this book.

opposite: Deja Thoris and Anna chat on Mark's bookcase. (photo by Chris Shellen)

For More about Marwencol

Visit

Website: www.marwencol.com
Facebook: www.facebook.com/marwencol
Twitter: twitter.com/marwencol

Watch

Marwencol
82-minute documentary directed by Jeff Malmberg
Available on DVD, Blu-ray, and Video on Demand in select markets

Read

Esopus magazine
Nonprofit arts journal featuring selected works by Mark Hogancamp
"Marwencol on My Mind," *Esopus* 5 (2005)
Esopus Artist Limited Edition (2014)
www.esopus.org
Editor: Tod Lippy

Contact

For inquires on sales and public exhibitions of Mark Hogancamp's artwork, contact:
One Mile Gallery
www.onemilegallery.com
onemilegallery@gmail.com
845.338.2035
Gallerists: Janet Hicks and Eddie Mullins

For publishing and media inquiries, contact:
Open Face, LLC
Media production company (documentary and books)
www.weareopenface.com
weareopenface@gmail.com

All information was current as of the printing of this book.